Hoover Institution Publications 139

Sir Donald Cameron: Colonial Governor

CONFERENCE
OF
SENIOR ADMINISTRATIVE OFFICERS
OCTOBER, 1929
GOVERNMENT HOUSE, DAR-ES-SALAAM.
TANGANYIKA TERRITORY.

STANDING .... C.H.A. Grierson (Lindi), A.E. Kitching (A.S.N.A.), I.S. Waterall (Lab. Commiss'r), F. Longland (Tanga).

SITTING .... G.F. Webster (Arusha), F.C. Hallier (Dar-Es-Salaam), T.G. Buckley, O.B.E. (Mwanza), P.E. Mitchell (S.N.A.)

SITTING R.A. Thompson (Iringa), A.H. White (Bukoba), H.C. Stiebel, O.B.E. (Tabora), Sir D.C. Cameron K.C.M.G., K.B.E. (Governor and Commander in Chief). (C.J. Bagenal, O.B.E. (Kigoma), Lt. Com'r A.M. Clark (Mahenge), H. Hignell (Do Doma).

Sir Donald Cameron
Colonial Governor

Harry A. Gailey

HOOVER COLONIAL STUDIES

Edited by
Peter Duignan and Lewis Gann

Hoover Institution Press
Stanford University
Stanford, California

Library of Congress Cataloging in Publication Data

Gailey, Harry A
    Sir Donald Cameron, colonial governor.

    (Hoover colonial studies) (Hoover Institution publications, 139)
    Bibliography: p.
    1. Cameron, Sir Donald, 1872–1948. I. Series.
II. Series: Stanford University. Hoover Institution on War, Revolution, and Peace. Publications, 139.
JV1009.C35G3   325'.342'09669 [B]   74–7301
ISBN 0-8179-1391-2

Hoover Institution Publications 139
International Standard Book Number 0-8179-1391-2
Library of Congress Catalog Card Number 74-7301
© 1974 by the Board of Trustees of the
      Leland Stanford Junior University
Printed in the United States of America

To H. G. and D. W. G.

IN MEMORIAM

Table of Contents

Preface

to the

African Colonial Studies Series

The last three decades or so have seen a revolution
in the historiography of modern Africa. Historians once
devoted their attention largely to the conquerors and
builders of empire; their colonial subjects went mainly
unrecorded. Then the pendulum started to swing the other
way. Imperial history began to fall from academic favor.
Scholars attempted to write the annals of modern Africa
in African terms, with the colonial period no more than a
cruel but short-lived interlude. Some academicians went
even further. The historians of Africa were to assume a
political mission: they were to assist in nation-building
and to lend their skills to bring about the triumph of a
particular ideology or a particular class. The term "Euro-
centric" became a word of abuse beloved by reviewers anx-
ious to denigrate those authors whose political philosophy
they happened to dislike.

Yet the history of the Europeans in Africa cannot be
separated from the history of Africa at large. No reput-
able historian of Eastern Europe, for instance, would deny
historical legitimacy, say, to a study of the Ottoman
conquerors of Albania or the Austrian invaders of Bosnia.
Similarly, the policies of a British governor in what is
now Tanzania or the exploits of a Belgian military leader
in what is now Zaïre belong to the history of Africa just
as much as they belong to the annals of Great Britian or
of Belgium, respectively.

Students concerned with the history of the Europeans
in Africa, moreover, enjoy advantages today that were not
available to their predecessors half a century ago. A
mass of new archival material has recently become acces-
sible in depositories both of the former metropolitan
powers and of the independent African states. In addition,
colonial historians can now draw on a great body of socio-
logical and anthropological material largely unavailable in
the early days of European colonization.

To take advantage of this new material and to reanalyze
the colonial period as a phase of Euro-African history, the
Hoover Institution has launched a new program of scholarly
inquiries organized around the theme of African Colonial
Studies.

One major series, directed by Peter Duignan and Lewis H. Gann, will deal with the men who modernized Africa-- Agents of Empire. This project, interdisciplinary in approach, will cover all colonial powers in sub-Saharan Africa. It will be concerned with the transference to Africa of Western institutions and modes of production, techniques and skills, ideas and ideals--in short, with the total Western impact on Africans. The project will seek to answer the following questions: What were the situations faced by the agents of colonialism both in their efforts to govern Africans and in their ideological justifications for doing so? How did African societies react and respond to foreign rule? What effects did Europeans have on African societies? What were the sequences of adjustment and change?

Five volumes are to be written by the general editors on: the administrators, the military and police, the businessmen, the technicians (e.g., engineers, doctors, scientists, and veterinary, agricultural, and forestry specialists), and the intellectuals (missionaries, teachers, academicians, writers, and opinion-makers).

Complementing this project will be a series of monographs about specific colonial administrators, soldiers, missionaries, companies, and other empire builders, as well as edited versions of primary sources (diaries and journals). We have also planned a volume of contributed essays on notable colonial governors as well as one on Belgian governors of the Congo. We are fortunate in being able to initiate this series with Professor Harry Gailey's study of Sir Donald Cameron, a British administrator whose work was so pivotal in shaping policies and practices in British Africa.

We trust that this and subsequent studies will help to elucidate and reinterpret the colonial past of Africa.

Peter Duignan

Lewis H. Gann

About This Book

Sir Donald Cameron is the first effort to analyze the totality of Cameron's contributions to British imperial administration in the 20th century. Tracing Cameron's public career from its beginnings in Guiana until his retirement as Governor of Nigeria, it covers his service under Lugard and Clifford in Nigeria, his important governorship of Tanganyika, and finally his return to Nigeria following the women's riots there.

Cameron's real education in colonial administration began with his assignment to Nigeria in 1908, where he worked under Sir Walter Egerton, Sir Frederick Lugard, and Sir Hugh Clifford. While the conventional wisdom asserts that Cameron learned his commitment to indirect rule from Lugard, the author believes that Cameron was, in fact, no great devotee of Lugard's system of indirect rule and that Clifford was much more influential in shaping Cameron's viewpoint toward government.

In 1924, Cameron was appointed governor of Tanganyika, where his first priority became the restructuring of the Native Authorities, whereby traditional African rulers could have a larger share in local administration. In pursuit of this goal he contended, with fair success, with two very sticky problems. First, the ultimate authority in Tanganyika was not totally clear. The British had gained control over Tanganyika through a League Mandate after World War I, and there was considerable debate over the roles of the League of Nations and the mandating power. Secondly, there existed in England and in neighboring Kenya a strong desire for a union of Tanganyika, Kenya, and other elements of British East Africa, a union which would have compromised Cameron's plans for African participation in government.

Returning to Nigeria in 1931, this time as Governor, Cameron again found serious impediments to his efforts to reform the Native Authorities. The depression and the accompanying need to master the intricacies of finance and to find ways to cut the cost of government seriously modified Cameron's plans. As in Tanganyika, Cameron, nevertheless, managed to overcome his immediate problems and move towards greater native autonomy, particularly in the troubled eastern areas. He had less success in the highly stratified northern Emirates.

As with many reformers, Cameron was aloof and made many enemies throughout his life. But he was a prodigious worker and an able administrator, and he used his talents and energies to substantially increase native autonomy in key areas of the British Empire.

Harry Gailey is a Professor of History and Coordinator of the African Studies Program at San Jose State University. He was selected Outstanding Professor at San Jose State for 1971-72 and he has received grants from the Ford Foundation, the Social Science Research Council, and the American Philosophical Society.

He has published five books on Africa, of which the most recent are History of Africa from 1800 to the Present (Holt, Rinehart and Winston, 1973) and History of Africa from Earliest Times to 1800 (Holt, 1970).

xi

Acknowledgements

The research for this book was done over a period of years. That related to Nigeria was completed in 1967 under the auspices of a grant from the Social Science Research Council. In this connection I wish to thank all those persons in Nigeria who aided me, particularly the Chief Archivist and his staff at the Federal Archives, Ibadan, and the staff of the University Library. My gratitude goes also to Dr. Robert Armstrong of the African Institute and to Professor J. F. Ade Ajayi and Dr. S. M. Tamuno of the History Department at the University of Ibadan. The late Professor J. C. Anene and Dr. A. E. Afigbo of Nsukka were also very helpful.

A further grant from The American Philosophical Society in 1971 combined with a sabbatical leave from San Jose State University, San Jose, California, enabled me to complete research on Cameron's activities in East Africa. As usual the Public Record Office, London, was a model of efficiency, and I wish to express my gratitude once again to its very competent personnel who assisted me. The staff of the Commonwealth Relations Library and the British Museum were also very helpful. Mr. J. J. Tawney of the Colonial Records Project, Oxford, rendered great assistance by helping me trace a number of Cameron's former associates. He was also most kind in sharing with me his reminiscences of Cameron and of service in Tanganyika in the late 1920s. Dame Margery Perham, one of the most knowledgeable persons on the theory and practice of British administration in Africa, interrupted her busy schedule to discuss at some length her remembrances of Sir Donald and his relationship with Lord Lugard. In addition to the debt we all owe her for her pioneering work, I thank her for some fresh insights into Cameron's complex personality. Dr. Anthony Sillery of Oxford University, formerly an administrative officer in Tanganyika, devoted time to answering my questions, and I remember with pleasure the long afternoon conversation we had on the subject of British administrative policy.

All of the persons who responded to my detailed inquiries concerning Cameron did so in detail. Many of them expressed great satisfaction that, however limited the biography would be, someone was at last concentrating directly upon the totality of Sir Donald's career. I wish to express my sincere thanks for their lucid and informative accounts and their permission to quote from some of their correspondence. The following list of those who helped me is a roster of long distinguished service to the British African empire: Nicholas Assheton, Sir Alan Burns, Sir John Nicoll, Dame Margery Perham, J. Rooke Johnston, G. S. Sayers, Dr. Anthony Sillery, Sir Rex Surridge, and J. J. Tawney. I hope that in a modest fashion I have done justice to their expectations and provided some insight into the career of one of the few great British colonial governors of the twentieth century.

                                        Harry A. Gailey

Los Gatos, California
7 July 1972

Glossary

Akida: the title of an Arab or Swahili administrative
    official in the coastal areas of Tanganyika who before
    the European occupation had jurisdiction over a group
    of villages. The Germans modified the position of the
    Akidas by making them a part of the administrative
    hierarchy with the responsibility of governing units of
    approximately 25,000 persons. Their authority was all
    but removed by Cameron's revision of the Native Authority
    system.

Alafin: the title of the ruler of the Yoruba state of Oyo.
    In the eighteenth century he was the most powerful ruler
    in Nigeria, but the civil wars of the nineteenth century
    reduced his influence to only the areas adjacent to
    the new city of Oyo. Even at the height of his power,
    the Alafin's authority was modified by a complex social,
    economic, and bureaucratic structure.

Alake: the title of the traditional ruler of the Egba state
    of Abeokuta. Between 1893 and 1914 he was the consti-
    tutional monarch of a semi-independent state where real
    executive authority was in the hands of ministers. In
    1914 Abeokuta was incorporated into Nigeria, and Lord
    Lugard vested great authority in the Alake. This action
    led eventually to the June 1918 uprising at Abeokuta
    where over 500 persons were killed.

Alkali: the title given to the official in a northern Niger-
    ian emirate whose chief responsibility was the adminis-
    tration of justice. Many of these officials retained
    their justice-dispensing roles after Lord Lugard's re-
    organization of the North. All the Class A or upper
    echelon Native Courts in Nigeria were Alkali courts.

Awujale: the title of the paramount ruler of the Ijebu
    people of western Nigeria. The actions of an Awujale
    in 1891-92 prompted one of the few British punitive
    expeditions sent against the people of western Nigeria
    and resulted in the incorporation of Ijebuland into
    the Lagos Protectorate.

Colonial Secretary describes two different administrative
    positions. It is often used to denote the minister
    in charge of the Colonial Office, the Secretary of
    State for Colonies, as well as describing the official
    in a British colony or protectorate who is in charge
    of the central Secretariat.

Eleko: the title of the hereditary ruler of Lagos. In the late nineteenth and early twentieth centuries, the Eleko was from the House of Docemo, the pliant ruler during the mid-nineteenth century who ceded Lagos to the British in 1861.

Gombololas: the courts of sub-chiefs among the Bukoba of Tanganyika.

Jumbe: the title given to a village headman during the period of German rule in Tanganyika.

Laibon: a Masai elder who reportedly had great magical or supernatural powers. Although he was a unifying force in the fragmented Masai society, he was in no sense the ruler of the group. However, early British administrators imagined his secular power to be greater than it was and invested him with considerable political authority.

Liwale: the Arab or Swahili appointed by the Germans to administer certain important cities or districts in Tanganyika. They were superior to and administered the activities of the Akidas in their districts.

Lukiko: the Bakama (chiefs) Courts among the Bukoba of Tanganyika.

Minute Paper: an addendum sheet which accompanied every major dispatch on its route through the Colonial Office. On it clerks, the Permanent Undersecretary, and in some cases the Secretary of State, would make notes and comments concerned with problems raised by a governor in his dispatch.

Native Authority referred to a unit of local government which could exercise executive, legislative, and financial control over a specific territory. Its functions were normally separate from those of Native Courts although members of a Native Authority usually were also included in the composition of a Native Court. At first the majority of Native Authorities were chiefs, either traditional or synthetic such as the Warrant Chiefs of eastern Nigeria. After the 1920s the tendency was more to recognize Councils rather than a single individual.

Native Courts were courts designed by the British which were composed primarily of Africans. Native Courts could be minor or major grade courts. The minor courts exercised jurisdiction over a small area and a restricted number of civil or criminal cases. Major courts had more authority and at times also had appellate jurisdiction over minor courts.

Warrant Chiefs were those Native Authorities created by the British in eastern Nigeria in the early twentieth century. They were given much more executive authority over a much larger area than had ever been the case of traditional political leaders in Iboland and parts of Ibibio territory. They also exercised much influence over the Native Courts of eastern Nigeria. Despite evidence to the contrary, British administrators continued to view the Warrant Chiefs as traditional rulers until the womens' riots of 1929.

Waziri: the highest officer of the bureaucracy in many Muslim states. His position approximated that of a Prime Minister as he was the general advisor to the ruler in most executive matters. The Waziri was particularly knowledgeable in legal affairs.

Early Career and Nigerian Developments

Some public men seem so assured of their place in history that they do everything possible to facilitate the work of historians of later generations. Memoranda, notes, speeches, and letters are all kept and in some cases their authors take care to see that these are neatly and efficiently indexed. It has been the habit in Britain for over a hundred years for many of its policy-makers to devote a large portion of their retirement to the preparation of memoirs or histories of their time. It is thus possible for later researchers with a minimum of difficulty to get at the raw material on which any personalized account of substance has to be based. By contrast, a very few government officials for wholly private reasons refuse either to admit that what they have accomplished would be of great concern to future generations or that their roles were important. They do not leave behind large dossiers of well-cataloged papers nor do they reminisce at great length about their private or public lives. In this respect the two dominant figures in the administration of British Africa in the twentieth century, Lord Frederick Delatry Lugard and Sir Donald Charles Cameron, are studies in contrast.

Lord Lugard, until his death over thirty years after his retirement from the Colonial Service, worked under the full glare of public scrutiny. He wrote one major book, <u>The Dual Mandate</u>, which stated in easily comprehensible form his concepts of colonial rule. Lord Lugard served as the British representative to the Permanent Mandates Commission of the League of Nations from 1923 until 1936. In addition he wrote numerous articles, attended conferences, gave lectures, and maintained a voluminous correspondence. Thus when Dame Margery Perham came to write Lugard's biography, she had a plethora of private papers, books, and articles as well as those official communications Lugard had dispatched to his superiors. In her excellent biography she was able to touch the surface of Lugard the man, detailing some of his private hopes, fears, and desires.

Sir Donald Cameron, who stamped his concept of government authority and responsibility upon British Africa even more firmly than did Lugard, left behind no collection of private papers. After his retirement from the Colonial

Service in 1935 he made few public appearances. The Conservative government, perhaps in deference to his growing blindness or perhaps in memory of his close friendship with the Labour Party, did not often use him in any major advisory capacity. Always withdrawn and with few close friends, the tragedy of his wife's long illness and his own growing infirmity drove him to even greater reticence. Few Londoners living close to Cameron's apartment in Sloane Street would have suspected that their tall, nearly blind neighbor was one of the molders and shapers of British colonial policy. Cameron's one book, My Tanganyika Service and Some Nigeria, was composed mainly of reworded earlier speeches and memoranda, held together by the threads of memory.[1] Although a mine of information for anyone who knows something of Cameron's career, the book is haphazardly organized and does not fully reflect Cameron's high, tightly structured intelligence.

The result to the potential biographer is the same whether Cameron planned to leave little behind for the prying eyes of historians or whether he merely did not consider it important to preserve a record of his career. It is impossible for anyone to write a complete, satisfactory biography of the man. Today there are questions which could only have been answered, perhaps, twenty years ago by close acquaintances now deceased. But the documentary evidence for his administration in Tanganyika and Nigeria remains and has been used for the many articles and books that relate the generalities of Cameron's administrative reform. However, no one has attempted to view these in the context of Cameron's developing career and relate one segment to another. Reading some historical and political accounts, one is left with the feeling that colonial administrations were disembodied, self-generating entities. However detailed these analyses are, they present the finished product of a reform with little or no reference to the contribution of the individuals involved. Although the usual type of biography of Cameron cannot be written, one can, nevertheless, constantly be aware of the interaction of the personality and intelligence of this extraordinary man on the events of his time. This is what a political biography should do, and although the absence of relevant data is frustrating, one can piece together enough of his personal life to give a better understanding of Cameron's public actions spanning a period of forty-five years of imperial service.

When Cameron was appointed Governor of Tanganyika at the age of fifty-three, many of his colleagues discovered that he was not an ordinary government appointee. Most governorships were reserved for men of the "right type." This generic phrase is very difficult to define, but most of those appointed to high positions were easily recognized as possessing certain qualities in common. Most colonial governors of the early twentieth century were of a solid middle- or upper-class background. They had normally received good education in excellent schools in England and, in addition to any administrative talent they might acquire, they had good connections. Many of them had military backgrounds. In the period before 1914 military leaders were necessary during and immediately after the occupation of territory throughout Africa. During the four-year bloodbath of World War I many more administrators were introduced to the profession of arms. Given the shortage of men in the colonial service after the war and the scarcely disguised system of political patronage, governors of African territories did not need to have had long experience in governing overseas territories. Most governors in British Africa had little knowledge of the areas they governed and some had no knowledge whatever of Africa and its multiplicity of peoples and cultures. A quick glance at some of the most important governors immediately after World War I, for all their later records, will show how few had administrative experience in Africa when appointed. Sir Hugh Clifford was drawn from the Malayan service, Sir Graeme Thomson had been a brilliant administrator of transport during the war, and Sir Gordon Guggisberg was a Brigadier of Engineers, though he had at least done survey work in West Africa. Sir Horace Byatt's most prestigious position had been as an administrator in Malta. Lord Lugard's training was that of a soldier, and Sir Edward Grigg's service had been either military or in direct secretarial service to the royal family. As will be seen, Sir Donald Cameron did not conform to the ordinary pattern of high colonial officials.

Cameron's early life is shrouded in mystery, but that he had an unusual childhood will be apparent to anyone who looks behind the dry facts that are available.[2] He was born on a moderate-sized plantation in Demerara, British Guiana, on 3 June 1872. His father and namesake was Donald Charles Cameron and his mother was the former Mary Emily Brassington of Dublin, Ireland. When he was still young the family abandoned plantation life and moved to Georgetown. Shortly afterward Cameron's mother died and he was sent to live with his grandparents in Ireland. The bulk of his formal education was obtained there at Rathmines School in Dublin. While it is almost impossible to state with accuracy the quality, or for that matter the quantity, of educational experience obtained by the young Cameron, it is certain that by comparison with his later colonial associates, his formal education was slight. This makes even more remarkable his later grasp of local government, legal systems, and finance, and his

3

ability to write clearly and succinctly which placed him among the leading Colonial Office practitioners of this craft. Cameron's lack of formal education and his later mastery of the discipline necessary to administer a territory was noted by all those who served with him. Sir Philip Mitchell, Cameron's brilliant Secretary for Native Affairs in Tanganyika, noted that Cameron "was largely self-educated, and if one may judge by the results he must have been a brilliant teacher."[3] Sir Donald's education clearly did not extend beyond the secondary level since it is known that he was living in the Caribbean area at the age of seventeen. At that time Cameron was working as a volunteer sorter in the Post Office of British Honduras during the Christmas rush, a post from which he was soon discharged after an altercation with a fellow worker. By early 1890 he had secured a position as a junior clerk in the Inland Revenue Department in British Guiana, and in the following year he transferred to the Colonial Service, becoming a fifth-class clerk in the Secretariat. These appointments, although far from prestigious, indicate that Cameron had some kind of local support since appointments to such positions were often amenable to local pressure.[4]

The last decade of the nineteenth century was obviously very important for the young Cameron. Unfortunately, little is known of the details of his life during these crucial years except that he advanced steadily in the service after 1895, becoming a third-class and dispatch clerk in that year, and being promoted to second-class clerk in 1899. He served as the private secretary to the acting governor in 1896, 1897, 1898, and again in 1901. This modest rise in a period of ten years from the lowest status clerk to the higher levels of the Secretariat of a second-class colony was not startling or unusual. However, it indicates a growing acquaintance with the details of administration and probably the mastery of its intricacies for which Cameron later became famous. Another trait of Cameron's later years, the habit of long working hours, was probably also developed at this time as was his abrasive, brusque manner which tended to offend people and insured that they did not invade his privacy. In Guiana Cameron was learning the fundamentals of his profession, something almost entirely lacking in many colonial governors.

For over a decade Cameron had performed ably in junior positions and his success had been largely of his own making. He had no important connections either in the West Indies or in England who could use their influence to his advantage. To operate without influence during the golden age of the British Empire was normally to condemn oneself to a life of mediocre positions. Fortunately by 1900 Cameron, presumably because of his administrative skills, had found someone who was willing to help advance his career. Sir Cavendish Boyle, the Governor of Guiana, although he did not possess great influence in England, nevertheless could help promote persons in those areas over which he had direct control. Thus, partly because of his own talent and partly because of Boyle's friendship, Cameron was appointed in 1900 secretary and clerk to both the Executive and Legislative Councils of the colony. In that year he also served very briefly as Acting Assistant Governor, the second highest position in the colony. In 1901 he became the principal clerk in the Secretariat. Fortune continued to be kind to him even after Boyle had left Guiana to become Governor of Newfoundland. In 1902 Cameron spent his leave in Newfoundland, presumably at Boyle's request, acting as the governor's private secretary, and when Boyle was appointed Governor of Mauritius in April 1904, he requested Cameron's transfer to that Secretariat. In July of the same year Cameron became the Assistant Colonial Secretary of Mauritius. During the absence of Sir Graham Bower from December 1904 until October 1905 and from April to September 1906, Cameron assumed charge of the entire Secretariat as the Acting Colonial Secretary. In June 1907, while Cameron was again acting in place of Bower, Governor Boyle requested the Colonial Office to confirm Cameron as Colonial Secretary if Bower found it impossible to return to Mauritius. Boyle reminded his superiors of Cameron's "tact and ability" which had been proved by his long service. The reply of the Colonial Office, while noncommittal, assured Boyle that Cameron would be given serious consideration for the position if the occasion ever arose.[5]

By the age of thirty-five Cameron had achieved a small measure of success. He had risen largely by his own merits from the lowest levels of West Indian administration to a position where he was recognized even by the officials of the Colonial Office as an extremely competent mid-range administrator. He could reasonably expect to continue to advance in the service, perhaps ultimately to be selected as the chief administrative officer in the Secretariat of a major British territory. It is doubtful whether Cameron's ambitions at this time extended beyond such modest goals. Even these were threatened by the events of July and August 1907.

Before detailing the first public crisis in Cameron's career it would be well to digress briefly to consider comments on some of Cameron's personal characteristics. Although these observations were made much later, they can be assumed to be reasonably correct with regard to this period of Cameron's life since an individual's personality has become fairly fixed by his mid-thirties. All accounts agree that Cameron was very thin and was over six feet tall. He was far from handsome; one of his acquaintances has stated that he was "very ugly" with a large head and a beaked nose surmounted by the glasses upon which he became increasingly dependent. His longtime associate in East Africa, Philip Mitchell, wrote that Cameron liked to be thought of as a strong, harsh man and always took pains to try and create such an image of himself, despite the fact that he was "gentle by nature, rather shy and kind hearted to a fault."[6] Mitchell further noted that Cameron had strong likes and dislikes and "he would say the most outrageous and even ill-natured things about people he didn't like. He had a whimsical and caustic wit particularly when dealing with people who had an over-inflated sense of their own importance."[7] Even the Governor of Kenya, Sir Edward Grigg, who opposed Cameron on many major items concurred with Mitchell that Cameron in private was shy, self-effacing, and did not like publicity.[8] However, Cameron, possibly because he had always had to fend for himself, was a supreme individualist and to many casual observers appeared harsh and egotistical. He was brilliant and extremely efficient, and respected such qualities in others. He made enemies, but few friends, although many of those who worked closely with him remembered him a generation after his death as one of the truly great men they had ever met.

All observers agree with Sir Alan Burns' statement that Cameron "had a remarkable capacity for work, a quick grasp of essentials, an astounding memory for details, and a facility for lucid expression in writing and speech."[9] He was ruthlessly efficient and demanding of himself and his subordinates. In later life his habit was to work through the day and late into the night; as Governor of Tanganyika he had no private secretary as such and even did his own typing. Aside from an occasional game of billiards or bridge, Cameron seems not to have developed any hobbies or even great interest in anything unconnected with his work.[10] Entertaining was one of the tasks of high office that he seemed never to enjoy. He always preferred small gatherings of people he knew and whose company he enjoyed. Those who were invited over and over again to Government House, first in Tanganyika and later in Nigeria, were a varied group whose common qualities seem to have been their intelligence and congeniality.

A factor in Cameron's personality which is extremely hard to evaluate but which was important in helping him keep his perspective, was his sense of humor. In his book he delights in relating some comment he made to the discomfiture of some overpompous official or subordinate. Most of these stories are not really very funny, but it is obvious that Cameron believed they were. Judith Listowel

6

tells how Cameron was amused by the zealous activity of a district officer in Tanganyika who, without the knowledge of the railway officials, had appropriated materials from the railroad which he had used to build a bridge.[11] J. Rooke Johnston recalls that some of Cameron's close associates in Tanganyika did not stand so much in awe of him that they did not joke with him about some of his weaknesses. He relates one interchange with Philip Mitchell:

> Cameron had a good eye for a 'pretty skirt.' On his visits to the various stations and districts he used to ask these good looking wives of junior officers if he could help them in any way, as life was rather austere. He asked one attractive woman if he could get her anything. She informed him that she would like a porcelain enamel bath instead of the galvanized iron coffins usually issued to outstations and Cameron promised her she should have it. Some six weeks later in Dar Es Salaam Cameron phoned P. E. Mitchell in the Secretariat and asked if Mrs. (X) had her bath yet. Whereupon P. E. M. replied, 'I do not know, Sir, water is short in that district at this time of year, but I will try and find out if she has bathed yet.'[12]

Cameron replied to this jibe, "You would try and be funny on a Monday morning." This exchange does not necessarily display great wit, but it does indicate clearly that Cameron's austere formal presence concealed a man who was capable of enjoying humor even when directed at him by a subordinate.

Cameron was married at the age of thirty-one just before leaving Guiana for his new position in Mauritius. The future Lady Cameron was Gertrude Gittens, a resident of Oldbury, Barbados. Despite much later speculation that Cameron's marriage was not totally satisfactory, it was a union which lasted almost forty-five years. That Cameron was devoted to his wife seems clear from a close reading of his book or a perusal of his first will written when Lady Cameron had been ill for some time and was then hospitalized. It is undoubtedly true, as many observers have noted, that Lady Cameron was a quiet, introverted woman who much preferred to remain in the background and who did not thrive on the many social functions that the wife of a governor had to perform. She appears not to have been Cameron's intellectual equal, but there were few who could make this claim. As Governor of Tanganyika, Cameron tended to invite certain couples over and over to small informal parties at Government House. In most cases the wives were charming and witty and the governor obviously enjoyed their company. But there was never a hint of scandal and it is obvious that Cameron's marriage was at least satisfactory.[13] Thus the charge by Sir Edward Grigg that Cameron was a lonely man during the crucial years of 1926-27 must be measured by an understanding of the different interpretations of the term lonely. The Camerons had one son, Geoffrey Valentine. To Sir Donald's great sorrow, his son who was then Legal Secretary to the Malta government was killed in an aircraft which disappeared in the Mediterranean in May 1941. This tragedy obviously affected Lady Cameron greatly and her condition which later required continuous hospitalization can be said to date from the loss of their only son.

The traits of individualism, honesty, and outspokenness, so clearly mentioned by Cameron's associates, almost ended his career in 1907 just when it appeared to be gathering momentum. The incident that precipitated such a crisis was relatively insignificant for everyone except Cameron, a few native Mauritians, and Cameron's friend and protector, Governor Sir Cavendish Boyle. The Colonial Office had selected as Receiver General of Mauritius an experienced officer, G. A. L. Banbury, who, however, was not a Mauritian. His appointment was resented by a number of Mauritian politicians who believed the position should have been reserved for someone born on the island. On 9 July 1907, Cameron, as Acting Colonial Secretary, chose to defend the government's position in a speech before the Council of Government. Some Mauritian politicians claimed that Cameron had singled out the Mauritian segment of the civil service for attack. Even though Cameron at a further meeting of the Council denied any such intention, some Mauritians supported by the local press shifted their attention from the question of the appointment of the Receiver General to Cameron's speech and demanded that the governor remove him immediately from office. Public meetings and threatening speeches convinced Governor Boyle that he was faced with a potentially riotous situation unless his former protégé was removed, and he so informed the Colonial Office by telegram on 24 July.[14] Cameron, on his part, told Governor Boyle that he would do whatever the governor believed necessary to restore order to the government.

Colonial Office personnel in London, removed by thousands of miles from the crisis, took a more detached view. They instructed Boyle that Cameron was not to resign until the Colonial Office had examined the offending speech very carefully. Charles Lucas, the Assistant Secretary of State, after reading the speech, noted in a minute of 26 August that "Mr. Cameron's remarks were very unfortunate, the more so because they happened to be true."[15] But by that date, after much communication between the Colonial Office and the governor, Cameron was allowed to depart from Mauritius on leave. This was Governor Boyle's decision since he believed that he could never restore order as long as Cameron was still on the island. The Colonial Office was disappointed in the governor, believing that he had mishandled the case by succumbing to local pressure. However, Boyle was not removed from office and his resignation was refused, since it was necessary not to allow the Mauritians a further victory. In writing the closing minute on the affair on 3 October, Lucas found that Cameron, although correct, had been indiscreet. But Governor Boyle's actions had precluded Cameron being sent back to Mauritius, and it was decided to keep "Mr. Cameron on leave until he can be sent elsewhere." One Colonial Office clerk noted about Cameron's next posting, "a little delay will do no harm."[16]

The little delay lasted for over four months. Over thirty years later Cameron, who normally concealed his private attitudes, related in his book how impersonally he was treated by the Colonial Office staff in London. They would give him no indication whether or not they considered him guilty in the Mauritian affair. Nor did they give any hints as to his future posting.[17] Cameron could, with reason, consider that by his candor before the Mauritian Council he had presumed too much and had wrecked his chance of major advancement. It was a mistake he would not repeat again. While he presumably continued to be blunt and frank in private conversation, he never went beyond the limits prescribed by protocol for the office he held. Thus in the years of his association with Lugard in Nigeria, Cameron never openly or officially criticized his superior although he disagreed vehemently with some of the Governor-General's practices.

In January 1908, Cameron finally received his new assignment. He was posted to the Protectorate of Southern Nigeria as the Assistant Colonial Secretary. Although it is difficult to rank British territories as to their importance at the beginning of the century, Cameron's position was an obvious demotion. In Mauritius he was being seriously considered for the permanent appointment as Colonial Secretary, a position in which he had already distinguished himself in an acting capacity. Cameron was by no means starting over, but he knew nothing of Nigeria and its complex problems nor did he have friends in high places there who would help with his career. Thus in his late thirties, Cameron was being called upon to show once again his administrative skills.

In 1908 there were, officially, two large, separate British protectorates in Nigeria. The Protectorate of Southern Nigeria had been created only in 1906 by combining

the Lagos and Niger Coast protectorates. This artificial
creation had been accomplished by the governor, Sir Walter
Egerton, not because of any real economic or political affinities between the two territories, but simply to minimize
administrative duplication and save money. The western part
of the protectorate was dominated by the Yoruba people.
Throughout the nineteenth century they had wasted their once
great military and economic power in a bewildering series of
internecine conflicts. Political authority in this period
came to be exercised through the medium of city-states such
as Ibadan, Ilesha, Oyo, and Ogbomosho. From their base at
Lagos, acquired in 1861, the British peacefully extended
their authority over the Yoruba and Egba people in the decade
after 1893. In both the Yoruba and Egba societies there was
an easily recognizable economic and political hierarchy,
particularly in the Yoruba city-states. The great chiefs and
their councils were guaranteed by British political agents
that their positions and power would be recognized by the
new government. Eastward of the Yoruba lived the distantly
related Binis. The once great kingdom of Benin had been conquered by a British column only in 1897. After deposing the
king and looting Benin City of its works of art, the British
made political arrangements which left their African appointees at all levels considerable power.[18]
   East of the River Niger live a large number of peoples
who had never felt it necessary to create large kingdoms.
The most important were groups of village oriented people who
were later collectively known as the Ibo and Ibibio, which
implied a unity that in fact did not exist. Along the coast
between the Niger and Cross rivers the Ijaw and some of the
Ibibio had reoriented their societies in the eighteenth and
nineteenth centuries to create great trading cities such as
Calabar, Bonny, Brass, and later Opobo. Britian was the
major European trading partner with these states, first for
slaves and later palm oil. During the scramble for Africa
the British from their base in the Oil Rivers Protectorate
(later renamed the Niger Coast Protectorate) and from those
posts established by the Royal Niger Company slowly absorbed
these cities and their immediate economic hinterland. Military strength was used to force King Jaja of Opobo, Nana of
the Benin River, and some lesser rulers to accept British
suzerainty. However, Iboland was not subjugated until after
1902 when Governor Sir Ralph Moor sent the Aro Expedition,
a large-scale military force, into the interior, and, even
then, British military columns were operating in some of the
most distant parts of Ibo territory until as late as 1914.
It is important to note that many British administrators
considered the Ibo and Ibibio to be among the least advanced
people in West Africa. Their languages were very difficult

10

to master and few Englishmen ever penetrated behind the facade of what appeared to be simplistic religious and political systems to the bewildering complexity of their forms. Already when Cameron arrived in Lagos the eastern sections of the Protectorate of Southern Nigeria, although providing surplus funds which were used elsewhere, were looked down upon by high-level administrators. This continued to be the pattern for over twenty years.[19]

North of the Protectorate of Southern Nigeria was the newly acquired Protectorate of Northern Nigeria. In the period from 1900 through 1906, Sir Frederick Lugard, using a combination of guile, diplomacy, and force, had overawed the emirs of the great Hausa-Fulani and Kanuri states and made actual the theoretical limits imposed on British expansion by the Anglo-French Treaty of 1898.[20] There were many local differences between the city-states that comprised the northern protectorate, but they all had much in common. There were many "pagan" people in these areas, but political and economic power was concentrated in the hands of a Muslim majority in each state. Although never accomplished totally, the political ideal was a theocracy, particularly after the triumph in the early nineteenth century of the ideas of the great Fulani teacher and reformer, Usuman dan Fodio. The emirs of each city-state had a large, efficient, long-established bureaucracy which administered a highly sophisticated political and legal system. Different in form and modified by the rule of the political adventurer, Rabeh, the Kanuri kingdom of Bornu nevertheless was a further example of a centralized Islamic state.

The northern territories of Nigeria except for Sokoto and Kano were not conquered by British forces in the same sense as were many of the peoples of the southern areas. In order to avoid continuing conflict and unnecessary expense, Lugard had made sweeping promises to the Muslim rulers to gain their adherence to the new rule. The relatively high degree of administrative competence in the Islamic states coupled with the aristocratic code of the northern ruling classes made them an object of admiration by their British overlords. In few parts of Africa was a subject people and their institutions so respected and protected. This attitude toward the Hausa-Fulani and Kanuri rulers warped the ability of British administrators at all levels to compare objectively the northern territories with the southern areas. To Lugard and most of his successors the institutions of the North and the system of indirect rule developed there were superior to those of any other parts of West Africa. A conscious effort was made, particularly after 1912, to force the southern areas to conform, notwithstanding cultural and

11

institutional differences, to the northern model.

Donald Cameron, because of the responsible positions he held, became a part of the effort to remold the traditional systems of government to conform to Lugard's concepts of indirect rule. However, it was not until late in Lugard's administration that Cameron could be considered to have had a major role in the development of Nigerian policy. Until then he was always overshadowed by other officers whose advice, if any, Lugard sought before turning to Cameron. Cameron was an administrative expert at home in the Secretariat, and Lugard tended to discount such officers, preferring men who had considerable field experience. The period after unification of the North and South, important as it was for Nigeria, must therefore have been a frustrating time for Cameron, but he prudently did not criticize his superior at that time nor did he ever later commit to writing any intemperate judgments of Lord Lugard.

2

Deputy to Lugard and Clifford

By the time of Lugard's arrival in Nigeria in 1912, Cameron had once again become an important cog in the administrative machinery of what was now a major British territory. But he was just a part of that impersonal group of officers who were charged with making realities of the ideas of the Colonial Office and the governor. Undoubtedly he had learned from his Mauritian experience that a good administrative officer, like his counterpart on the General Staff, should remain anonymous. The governor of a British protectorate was the locus of authority. Removed from the direct control of his superiors in London and having their confidence, he set the tone for the entire administration. If Cameron had any significant disagreements with Sir Walter Egerton or his other superiors, he never recorded them in any fashion. He obviously admired Egerton for his administrative skills and his understanding of economics. In fact, Cameron believed that Nigeria owed more to Egerton in the area of economic development than to any other governor to have served the protectorates.[1] Although we know little of the details of Cameron's work under Egerton, it is obvious that his abilities were soon recognized since he was given more responsibility. He was promoted in 1911 to Principal Assistant Secretary and served most of the following year as Acting Colonial Secretary during the first few months of Lugard's administration. Also, in 1910 and again briefly in 1911 and 1912, Cameron was an Acting Provincial Commissioner in Warri Province of eastern Nigeria. This was the only time in his long career that he had direct field experience.

In March 1912, Sir Frederick Lugard returned to Nigeria after an absence of almost six years. He was given concurrent appointments as Governor of both the Protectorates of Northern and Southern Nigeria with the specific task of amalgamating the two territories. For over four years Lugard exercised an authority over Nigeria seldom given to a governor of a British colony or protectorate. This was largely due to the extreme trust, if not open deference, paid to him by Lord Harcourt, the powerful Colonial Secretary, in Asquith's Liberal government. A statement made by Harcourt to Lady Lugard in 1913 indicated this relationship very clearly:

> Your husband has an unrivaled experience in
> Africa. He is the greatest living authority on African

affairs. And I do assure you when the other members of the Colonial Staff come to me at the Office and want to disagree with something he has laid down I shrug my shoulders and say "I don't know, but I trust Lugard to know better than any of us and he must have his way."[2]

Another indication of Lugard's special status was the approval by the Colonial Office of a modified version of his "scheme." The original version had been worked out by Lugard in 1906 and agreed to by the Conservative Colonial Secretary, Alfred Lyttleton. The "scheme" very simply was a way by which Lugard could spend a large amount of time in England with his beloved wife, Flora, while still retaining full administrative control of affairs in Nigeria. One of the major reasons for Lugard's resignation as Governor of Northern Nigeria in 1906 was the failure of the Liberal Colonial Secretary, Lord Elgin, to honor his predecessor's promise concerning the "scheme." When Harcourt opened correspondence with Lugard in 1911 concerning a return to Nigeria, the "scheme" once more became an important issue. Eventually the Colonial Office approved Lugard's absence from Nigeria for four months of the year. During that time Lugard had a special office at the Colonial Office which he shared with his brother, Edward. All incoming mail from Nigeria was first delivered to them. They would work their way through the mass of correspondence, Lugard would make decisions, and he and his brother would then write the necessary type of dispatch justifying these. Only then would the Nigerian dispatches be sent to the regular officials in the Colonial Office.[3]

The impelling reasons behind the amalgamation of the two protectorates were economic. The North, landlocked and poor, was operating at a deficit. Its recurrent and development budgets were balanced by subsidies from the British government and by diverting funds from the more prosperous southern protectorate. It is ironic that the areas most ignored by Lugard and his successors were those whose economies were utilized to finance the development schemes in the North. To the Colonial Office there appeared to be unnecessary duplication of offices in all the branches of the civil service in the two areas. Railway construction provided another major reason for uniting Nigeria. The southern railway had reached Jebba by 1909 and plans were already in hand to extend it to Minna. This would place it in competition with the northern line and its proposed extension to Baro. Further, construction had begun on the eastern line which would pass through Enugu and eventually extend to the North. It seemed to government officials in London that amalgamation was the solution to effect greater budgetary savings while insuring more standardized rule for all the people of Nigeria.[4]

There is nothing to indicate that Lugard ever disagreed with the concept of amalgamation. Certainly he pursued the task with the singlemindedness so characteristic of the man. By May 1913, his detailed draft proposal had been completed and submitted to Lord Harcourt. After a very brief scrutiny, Lugard's plans were approved with only a few changes. Unification of the two protectorates became a reality on January 1, 1914, and Lugard became the chief administrative officer with the special, personal title of Governor-General.[5]

In accordance with Lugard's plans, the main administrative divisions between the North and South were retained after amalgamation. Central offices, such as the Judiciary, Police, Treasury, and the Railways, were established only where common problems in each area demanded the same policy. The lieutenant-governors of the North and South were responsible for the everyday administration of their territories with roughly the same freedom and responsibility they had exercised as governors. Only problems relating to Nigeria as a whole were to be referred to Lugard. This was, in theory, so that the Governor-General would be able to concentrate on the larger problems and so insure continuous reform of the system. A small central Secretariat was created ostensibly to facilitate decision making at the highest levels.

Donald Cameron was placed in charge of the Nigerian Secretariat and given the title of Central Secretary. He thus became one of the major architects of the new Nigerian policy. It is, however, important to note that Lugard was little influenced by the arguments of men who disagreed with him about a given policy. There is no evidence to indicate that Cameron ever openly opposed Lugard on any particular policy, not even on the haphazard way in which the central Secretariat was organized or Lugard's penchant for ignoring his own administrative system. In the formative years of Nigeria, Cameron remembering Mauritius, remained discreetly silent on even those items with which he was most closely concerned.

Even if Cameron had been inclined to oppose his superior, the example of Charles Temple, the lieutenant-governor in the North, would have been a lesson in the futility of such action. Temple, a man with great experience and knowledge of the North, was one of the few high officials who openly opposed Lugard's scheme of amalgamation. He believed that instead of unifying the two radically different areas, the Colonial Office should further subdivide the territory into perhaps as many as seven provinces to reflect tribal and religious differences more adequately. This opposition and

later his differences with Lugard over details of implementing indirect rule earned Temple nothing but criticism from
his superiors.[6] Temple was one of the major topics of conversation between Lady Lugard and Lord Harcourt in their many
teas à deux in London. She made it clear that the Governor-
General considered Temple one of the major obstacles to carrying out plans necessary for developing a healthy Nigeria.[7]
Such was Lugard's prestige that few suggestions made by Temple
were put into effect and he was considered a troublemaker by
the Colonial Office. It is significant that Temple received
no honors for his long service, and when he left Nigeria in
1917, he was given no further position in the Colonial Service.

     The government established after unification reflected
the ideas of the Governor-General to a much greater extent
than was normal in a British territory. Lugard did not believe that Nigeria had reached the point where a Legislative
Council could contribute constructively to the governance of
the country. It might, rather, become an impediment in the
way of the rapid changes he was contemplating. Thus the
Legislative Council whose powers had been extended to all
the southern protectorate in 1906 was restricted to act only
for Lagos Colony. Instead, Lugard created for the rest of
Nigeria the Nigerian Council which had a majority of official
members. Containing only six Africans, it was an unlikely
check upon the Governor-General's plans.

     After amalgamation the northern administration remained
relatively intact but that of the South was totally reorganized. Previously, provincial commissioners in the South had
been able to exercise the authority of de facto lieutenant-
governors. Now the three large provinces were abolished and
instead nine smaller provinces were created. These smaller
units were then subdivided into three or more districts. The
district officers remained the key to governing the protectorate, but Lugard's reforms made it harder for the complaints or suggestions of these officials to reach the highest
echelons of the administration.

     Lugard's name is inextricably connected with the concept
of allowing African rulers to retain a large portion of their
traditional systems of government and law. His influence on
the Colonial Office and his writings in defense of this system left many persons with the erroneous idea that Lugard
"invented" it. In fact, British administrations had been
using forms of indirect rule in India for centuries, while in
South Africa a most advanced type of indirect rule had been
put into practice by Theophilus Shepstone in governing Zulu
and other Ngoni groups in Natal in the 1840s. R. B. Llewellyn in Gambia, and Ralph Moor and George Goldie in Nigeria

had all predated Lugard in the use of highly sophisticated
systems of indirect rule. Lugard was, nevertheless, the most
articulate spokesman for indirect rule for over a generation,
and it has been presumed that Cameron learned the rudiments
of its administration from Lugard. The proving ground for
Lugard's early ideas on this method of government was Northern Nigeria. As Governor of the Northern Protectorate until
1906, he found that this was the most expedient way to rule
a huge territory with the men and money he had available.
Lugard was more fortunate than his southern contemporary,
Ralph Moor, in that he dealt with highly sophisticated, well-
articulated administrative structures. The Hausa-Fulani
systems had been evolved over several hundred years of practice and were based upon religious sanction as well as the
precedents of past administrative action.

Indirect rule as it existed in Nigeria prior to the
enactment of Lugard's legislation after 1912 tended to reflect the local differences between major African groups.
Government in the South as constituted by Moor and Egerton
had been created to meet the needs of the Ibo and Ibibio in
the East and the Yoruba in the West. The greatest flaw in
either of these administrations was that few Europeans in
the period 1895-1914 understood the traditional systems of
the Yoruba, much less the highly complex, decentralized Ibo
and Ibibio forms of law and government. With time these flaws
could possibly have been minimized, and Warrant Chiefs in
the East and town chiefs in the West who did not have popular
support could have been replaced by those who did. As it was,
Lugard's reforms made any such improvement much more difficult.[8]

Lugard did not understand or appreciate the diffuse cultures of the eastern peoples. His inclination, despite pronouncements to the contrary, was to look to the North for his
models. Even had he been more concerned with the Ibo and
Ibibio, there were few men in the service who knew their language or more than a smattering of their customs and beliefs.
These officers were normally too junior for their opinions to
count very heavily with their superiors in Lagos. Lugard was
suspicious of anthropologists and was instrumental in dis-
charging the only one employed by the Nigerian government.[9]
Thus the reforms instituted by the Governor-General were
reactions to earlier European legislation, never questioning
certain basic assumptions on which that legislation was
based.

One of Lugard's major acts of legislation was the Native
Courts Ordinance of 1914 which attempted to establish a standard system of courts for all Nigeria. It created four
grades and five different types of courts. The "A" grade
court was that of either a paramount chief and his advisors

17

or an alkali court. The majority of "A" grade courts were
in the North. The Ordinance affected the North very little,
since it merely confirmed the continuing operation of functioning major courts. The "B," "C," and "D" grade courts
were those of varying jurisdiction operated by lesser chiefs
or officials. In the East the highest courts were "B" grade,
though these accounted for only a few of the reconstituted
Native Councils. In a large part of the southern territory
the Native Court area was also the administrative unit, and
any substantial reform of the courts would also demand administrative reforms. This was not done. Even corruption and
poor administration were not directly attacked, although the
Ordinance attempted to curb the Native Court clerks' penchant
for bribery and extortion. Moreover, Lugard removed European
officers from presiding over meetings of Native Courts and
restricted them to acting only as advisors. District officers
were not to interfere unless a gross injustice was being
done.[10]

The Native Courts Ordinance also removed the Native
Courts from the jurisdiction of the Supreme Court. A supplementary act created a Provincial Court within each province
with concurrent jurisdiction with the Native Courts.[11] These
courts, under the presidency of the provincial officer (Resident), could also act as appellate courts. Some measures such
as these were needed, but Lugard's reforms went too far in
separating the African system of law and administration from
the European. What Lugard accomplished was to effect the
continuation, particularly in the South, of administrative
and judicial bodies which had little relation to traditional
structures, and he then attempted to protect them from interference by European officers on the ground of protecting indigenous systems from unwarranted interference.

Despite the fact that in most Nigerian societies the
executive and judicial functions were not separated, Lugard
envisioned an early division of these powers. To further
this desire, he issued a general Native Authority Ordinance
in early 1916.[12] Once again the North supplied the model
since a large segment of the judicial system there was outside the control of the chief executive authority of the
Hausa-Fulani states. But before any such separation could
take place anywhere in Nigeria it was necessary to have one
man or group of men whose executive authority was recognized
by the people over a wide area. Consequently, in western
Nigeria, Lugard and his successors attempted to bolster the
Yoruba chiefs by allowing them to exercise with few checks
a type of authority that in traditional society they had
shared with other religious and secular officials. In early
1916, Lugard introduced a Native Authority system for Oyo,

making the Alafin its head. His basic misconception was to
view the Alafin's authority as essentially the same as a
northern emir's. As a result of this misunderstanding, there
were demonstrations against the new system which climaxed in
October with the murder of two Oyo Native Authority officials
at the town of Iseyin. The spread of disorders throughout
Yorubaland was halted only by the swift dispatch of troops to
the affected areas.[13]

An even more serious rejection of Lugard's policies
occurred at Abeokuta which had been guaranteed semi-independ-
ent status by the Treaty of 1893. The government of this
Egba state had been modeled roughly on the British pattern
and the chief executive or Secretary had been guided by the
missionaries and the British Commissioner. Soon after his
arrival in 1912, Lugard made clear his distaste for such an
arrangement. Two years later he found his excuse for direct
intervention in the affairs of the Egba government in the
death in prison of one of the Secretary's opponents. Mild
demonstrations in different parts of Egba territory were
staged against the incumbent Secretary and the Alake asked
for British troops to maintain order. Further tension led
to the so-called Ijemo massacre where British troops fired
on dissidents. With the Alake's support Lugard abrogated the
1893 agreement and incorporated Abeokuta directly into the
protectorate.[14] The next development occurred four years
later when the Alake was constituted the Native Authority
and direct taxation was extended to Abeokuta. In mid-1918
the Egba rebelled against this dictated government and the
Alaka just managed to escape with his life. The Egba tore
up the railway lines, looted trains, and a number of persons
lost their lives. Over a thousand troops, many just returned
from the East African campaign, were sent to Abeokuta. In
the fighting that ensued over five hundred Egba were killed.[15]
This expensive protest movement was a direct result of
Lugard's attempt to force what he believed the correct "Native Authority" upon a people whose "traditional" system he
had violated. A Commission of Inquiry appointed by the Colonial Office to investigate the causes of the riots placed
the blame squarely upon Lugard's new policy.

In the East the diffused political system of the Ibo
and Ibibio defeated Lugard's plans for further centralizing
authority. Thus in that crucial area the Native Authority
Ordinance of 1916 was applied with only minimal effect. The
Native Court area continued to be the basic unit of government. Warrant Chiefs with little backing from traditional
leaders exercised, under the protection of British authorities, arbitrary power. The court clerks, because of their
education, continued to dominate the chiefs; in fact,
Lugard's reforms had made this easier by removing direct

European supervision from the courts. Unrest in the East simmered until late 1929 when the women's riots exploded the myth of indirect rule in Ibo and Ibibio territories.[16]

Judgment after the fact is always easy, and one must be very careful not to indict an administrator for not possessing clairvoyance. Lugard was sent to Nigeria to unify the two areas. This he did with dispatch, creating only minor dislocation in the existing methods of rule. The Colonial Office had implicit faith in him, and he justified that faith. After only a few months as Governor-General, during the most crucial period in establishing his new system, Lugard had to contend with a World War and the specific problem of reducing the power of the Germans in the Cameroons. Soon afterward he had to extend his already meager resources to provide a civil administration for the conquered area while at the same time having to live with shortages of all types caused by the war. The negative aspects of Lugard's policies in Nigeria have been stressed, not because they represent the totality or even the major part of his contribution, but because they presented problems with which his successors in office were forced to cope. The crises in Nigeria in the 1920s and 1930s were in large measure reflections of the inadequacies of Lugard's policies.

From a certain point of view, one can say that Sir Donald Cameron was a disciple of Lugard. In writing about Lugard's relationship with his Central Secretary, Margery Perham noted that,

> None was more valuable to him than Cameron who, with his clear, dry mind and his confident grasp of economic and financial realities was the perfect complement for Lugard's more subjective and temperamental approach.[17]

Too many observers, however, have noted only the positive aspects of their relationship and have agreed that later, as Governor of Tanganyika, Cameron was merely extending his master's system. Cameron learned from Lugard also in a negative fashion. Even in his earlier years as Governor of Tanganyika, he declaimed against the imposition of systems of rule upon Africans without first engaging in meticulous research to discover the basis of traditional authority. Such a firm conviction could only have been formed while serving in Nigeria and observing Lugard's handling of Southern Nigeria. More fundamental than any other disagreement with Lugard was Cameron's concept of the necessity for a well-organized, smoothly performing central administrative structure.

Lugard's theory that the Governor-General should deal
with only those items of importance for all of Nigeria very
soon became inoperative. This was attributable to two factors. The first was the lack of a large, well-trained central Secretariat which could have relieved the pressure on
the Governor-General. That Cameron was never able to con-
struct such an agency was due largely to the second factor--
Lugard's compulsion to deal personally with even the most
trivial matters. Lugard's biographer confirms this habit.
In one amusing aside, she relates how Lugard, while at the
Colonial Office in London, took time to write a memo in reply
to the request of a second-class administrative officer for
government issued chamberpots.[18] Sir Alan Burns, later to
become Governor of Nigeria, who worked in the Secretariat
while Lugard was Governor-General, remarked over thirty years
later,

> He was a great man and a great governor, but he
> was unable to leave details to his subordinates and
> wasted much of his time on trifling work that others
> could have done for him. As a result his desk was
> always crowded with papers through which he worked
> steadily but slowly. Many a time, at the suggestion
> of impatient Secretariat officers, I have moved an
> urgent file to the top of the pile of papers on his
> desk, only to find it replaced later in the exact
> position from which I had moved it.[19]

Some idea of the demands this made upon Lugard can be seen
by the complaint of his successor, Sir Hugh Clifford, that
to keep up with just the paperwork forced him to spend between 72 to 90 hours a week at his desk.[20]
     Most of the important work on the central level was
undertaken by Lugard with only a very small staff. He maintained this arrangement because he was afraid that with a
larger Secretariat he would loose his flexibility and be
chained to the capital. He believed a large, efficient
Secretariat would remove his freedom of action and perhaps
threaten his "scheme" which the Colonial Office honored until 1917. The Colonial Office disapproved of the lack of
a proper Secretariat but did not press the issue since both
Bonar Law and W. H. Long who succeeded Harcourt considered
their main problem vis à vis Lugard to be negating the "scheme."
Once Lugard's in absentia hold on the everyday administration
of Nigeria had been broken, then the Colonial Office could
begin to insist upon the creation of a more normal method of
administration.[21] However, little had been done in this direction by the time Lugard resigned as Governor-General in
1919.

Cameron in his book written in the mid-1930s was very reticent in discussing the shortcomings of his contemporaries, but he did note how unhappy he was with Lugard's _ad_ _hoc_ administrative system. Cameron had very strong opinions on subjects about which he knew a great deal. Administration was his forte, and one can imagine that if Burns was annoyed by Lugard's habits, Cameron must have been furious. He described Nigeria's administration as an attempt to rule with "no coordinating link save the memory of one man, the Governor, and that memory would naturally disappear with him when his term of office was concluded."[22]

Dame Margery Perham has remarked that she sensed a coolness between Lugard and Cameron in the 1920s and early 1930s. She attributed this in part to Lugard's sense of what was expected of a gentleman, and although Lugard never expressed it directly, there was the feeling that Cameron was not quite a gentleman.[23] Sir Donald, on his part, must have felt trapped in a system which revolved about one man. Knowing the shortcomings of Lugard's administration, he may have resented bitterly the well-meaning comments in the 1930s on how he had taken Lugard's ideas and applied them to Tanganyika. Rightly or wrongly, he believed that the Tanganyika system and later the reforms in Nigeria proceeded from his own concepts and owed little in practice to Lugard. However correct these speculations are about the later relations between the two men, Cameron was obviously not altogether content working under the direction of Lugard. He later commented that he would not have been unhappy before 1919 to have been transferred from Nigeria.

Lugard's departure from Nigeria allowed certain fundamental alterations to be made in the administrative structures, but his influence on the philosophy of African government remained powerful. From his vantage point as an author and lecturer, he, more than anyone else, gave to the pragmatic system of indirect rule an aura of near sanctity. As a member of the Permanent Mandates Commission of the League of Nations, he continued to exercise a profound influence upon Colonial Office officials at all levels. In Nigeria, contrary to Lugard's own stated views, many officials from the district level through to the central government came to view the protectorate government as static. Such was Lugard's prestige that lesser men either did not wish to challenge any of his dispositions or else gave up in the face of opposition from superiors who believed that the great man had made the final arrangements for the future of the African people. This attitude meant that in the North, where the symptoms were most pronounced, provincial and district officers did little to interfere with the near monopoly of decision making of the very conservative Muslim rulers. In less than a decade administrative officers there were treating the great emirs almost as if they were independent sovereigns. In the South the Lugard legacy of ignoring the actual traditional forms of rule became very pronounced during the administration of Governor Graeme Thompson and eventually led to the disastrous women's riots in the East in December 1929.

Lugard's successor, Sir Hugh Clifford who was appointed in July 1919, carried only the title of Governor since the more prestigious one of Governor-General had been reserved personally for Lugard only. This fact in itself indicates the differences in the administration of Nigeria in the 1920s compared with the Lugard years. The Colonial Office had reasserted its control and the governors, no matter how distinguished, were once more a part of a standardized system. While possessing great on-the-spot powers, Clifford understood that any major step had to be undertaken with the prior approval of the London officials if it was to succeed. They, in turn, did not stand in awe of him. There was no Harcourt to say that the governor always knew best. Such a state of affairs was not conducive to the creation of mythic heroes, but it was a necessary factor in the establishment of a good bureaucracy.

Sir Hugh Clifford, unlike most of his middle-class contemporaries in the Colonial Service, came from an aristocratic background. Born in 1866, he was the grandson of a peer and the son of a general who had won the Victoria Cross in the Crimean War. The family was Catholic and Sir Hugh was educated at private Catholic schools. He had been intended for the army, but instead, after passing the examination for Sandhurst, at the age of eighteen joined the Malay Civil Service. He very early distinguished himself and became the first British Resident to the Sultan of Pahang. Clifford became an expert on the Malay language, cooperating with Frank Swettenham to produce a Malay dictionary. In addition, he was the author of several novels of romance and travel. His second wife, Mrs. Henry de la Pasture, was also a novelist as was his stepdaughter, E. M. Delafield.

Sir Hugh left Malaya to become Governor of North Borneo in 1899. After many disagreements with the policy of the North Borneo Company, he resigned and returned to Malaya as a Resident. In 1905 he was appointed Colonial Secretary of Trinidad and in 1907 became the Colonial Secretary of Ceylon.[24] At the age of forty-six, in the same year that Lugard was sent to Nigeria as Governor-General, Clifford became Governor of the Gold Coast. The war prevented Clifford from undertaking substantial reforms in the Gold Coast, though he saw clearly the need to establish a more pragmatic but flexible administration and to educate British officers concerning African customs and behavior. Even if he could do little to improve native administration, his dispatches show that he was fully aware of what was wrong, and he did convince the Colonial Office to increase the size of the Legislative Council and appointed six Africans as members. He was also active in trying to reduce the differences in the civil service between Africans and Europeans. The commission Clifford appointed to make a complete survey of education in the Gold Coast made its report after his successor, Gordon Guggisberg, arrived at Accra. Guggisberg inherited from Clifford a sound economy and plans for the improvement of the roads, railroads, medical facilities, a secondary school at Accra, and a deep water port at Takoradi. Guggisberg's biographer has correctly underlined the debt that this most popular governor owed to Clifford. It is one of the ironies of the Colonial Service that both Guggisberg in the Gold Coast and Lugard in Nigeria have received credit for projects that originated in the highly developed mind of Sir Hugh Clifford.[25]

Sir Hugh had little time to acquaint himself with his new position as Governor of Nigeria before he was made painfully aware of the considerable dissatisfaction which existed in Nigeria among both the European and African civil servants. Representatives of the European civil servants, known by some as the "Bolshie Society," called upon the governor to stress the necessity of improvements in the conditions of service and salary schedules. Donald Cameron was a member of this deputation. Furthermore, the African Civil Service Union did not wait much longer than their European counterpart in complaining about the levels of African salaries. As a first step, the governor appointed Cameron to collect basic information from various departments concerning their functions, financial commitments, and complaints. Clifford then created two commissions to investigate conditions as outlined by the civil servants and to recommend alterations if they were needed. Cameron was appointed to supervise one of them, the Commission on Salaries. Thus began the cordial cooperation between Clifford and Cameron which within three years transformed the central administration of Nigeria.[26]

The two commissions made their reports in February 1920. That headed by Cameron was 123 pages long, thorough, and very detailed. It covered the whole range of complaints of the civil service with regard to salaries and promotions. Cameron proposed long-term changes in staffing, particularly at the central level, and improvements in the salaries of certain categories. Chief among his recommendations was a plan for clarifying the order of seniority of some of the more

24

senior officers. This problem dated from 1914 when amalgamation had required the combining of the civil services of the two protectorates.[27] Sir Hugh accepted most of the recommendations of the commission and praised Cameron's efficiency to the Colonial Office. The quick definitive moves by the new governor convinced the civil servants that Clifford would do everything possible to secure fair treatment of their grievances. However, the governor had to wait upon Colonial Office action for some of his reforms and this took considerable time. For example, as late as January 1922, he was still requesting his superiors to approve Cameron's suggestion concerning relative seniority of administrative officers of long service.[28] Eventually on February 9, 1922, Winston Churchill, then Colonial Secretary, made the decision to approve most of the governor's recommendations, and the issue of seniority was finally settled.

The problem which claimed the major part of Governor Clifford's time during the first half of his administration was the thorough redesign of the central administration. He communicated to the Colonial Office his disappointment on the state of the administration in early December 1919.[29] In May 1920, he complained about the slowness of his superiors in approving his proposals. Clifford endeavored to describe to the Secretary of State for Colonies, Lord Milner, "the defective character of the machinery which was devised under the amalgamation scheme for the transaction of business in Nigeria." He complained that despite a normal work week of over 72 hours at his desk he could not keep up with the paperwork which was forwarded to him from the northern and southern provinces as well as from the central administration. Adding to his burden of correlating three Secretariats was the lack of officers on all levels who possessed much experience in administration. Governor Clifford suggested that a remedy for this situation would be the creation of a single Secretariat and the establishment of the position of Secretary for Native Affairs.[30] The Colonial Office clerks betrayed their lack of knowledge of the situation when they acidly noted that Clifford could not be too efficient if he had to work so hard. Other comments were to the effect that Clifford was simply taking this way of trying to downgrade Lugard. Nevertheless, the Colonial Office by July 1920 gave Clifford the necessary approval to implement his schemes.

In this period of reorganization Clifford appears to have looked to Cameron as his major advisor rather than to senior field officers such as the Lieutenant-Governor of the Southern Provinces, Major Harry Moorhouse. Certainly proximity played a role in Clifford's decision, but Cameron also possessed administrative training matched by only a few

persons in the Colonial Service. It appears that there
quickly developed a close bond between the dour, efficient,
self-made Chief Secretary and his volatile, aristocratic
chief. Clifford made clear his reliance upon Cameron and his
complete trust in the results of Cameron's work in numerous
dispatches to the Colonial Office. While on leave in England
in mid-1920, Cameron acted as Clifford's representative to
the Colonial Office.[31]

The major portion of the work of investigating the totality of the Nigerian administrative system and making specific
recommendations for change fell upon Cameron and his small
staff. The detailed plans for a single Secretariat were presented to the governor in November 1920, and Clifford forwarded them to the Colonial Office early the following month.
Included in the dispatch transmitting the proposed changes
were two long memoranda from Cameron detailing African and
European staff requirements for the new system.[32] Cameron's
suggestions had been approved by Clifford and they were not
substantially modified by the Colonial Office. The single
Secretariat as proposed by Clifford went into effect on
1 January 1921, and Cameron was appointed Chief Secretary to
the government. For his work during this period of transition Cameron was made a Knight of the British Empire in early
1923.

After the creation of the single Secretariat the bulk
of Cameron's time was spent in supervising the everyday administration of an increasingly prosperous Nigeria. It was
in this position that he showed to the fullest the traits
that had earlier led Temple to brand him as "the Pushful
Secretary."[33] Cameron was concerned with creating an organization which could efficiently translate policy into reality.
In order to do this he had to take officers who had little
administrative experience and mold them into hard-working,
efficient, clearheaded administrators. He himself worked
long hours and assimilated huge masses of data in order to
arrive quickly at defensible decisions. These traits he also
expected in his subordinates. Sir Alan Burns, who was Cameron's deputy (and also an excellent historian), noted of
this period in the Nigerian Secretariat,

> We had to work very hard and for very long hours,
> and our work was measured by the very high standard
> set by our chief himself. He suffered no fool gladly
> and quickly got rid of those who failed to reach the
> standard. With Sir Hugh Clifford as Governor and Sir
> Donald Cameron as Chief Secretary, the staff of the
> Nigerian Secretariat received such a training as is
> seldom given to young officers.[34]

The success of Cameron's efforts can be measured in part by a note on a Colonial Office minute paper acknowledging the receipt of the Blue Book for 1921. The writer commented that "this report has arrived 8 months earlier than the 1920 one, so our remonstrances have had effect."[35] Discounting the typical Colonial Office smugness, one can see here the emergence of Cameron's reputation with the Colonial Office for his coolness, accuracy, and efficiency. Cameron was also beginning in Nigeria that systematic education of junior officers which would in itself have a profound effect upon the colonial system in Africa, since many of those who worked under his direction in the decade and a half after World War I later became colonial governors. Cameron's concept of how the Chief Secretary should operate mingled with his pride in the Nigerian Secretariat when he wrote,

> When I was Chief Secretary of Nigeria, before my transfer to Tanganyika, I had two senior officers with long Secretariat training and experience (they are both governors at the moment I write), each in charge of a section of the office; as they were extremely competent, I never saw detail as a general rule and the cases which came up to me were properly and adequately digested and prepared. I was thus left with time to perform my legitimate duties, although I worked long hours.[36]

After the reorganization of the central administration, Sir Donald was unquestionably the number two man in the government. His analytical mind and self-effacing actions as an administrator complemented Sir Hugh's brilliant but volatile leadership. Cameron served as acting governor during Clifford's absence in 1921, 1923, and 1924. This was no titular position as it might have been with Lugard. The decisions Cameron made were his own, and it is indicative of the closeness of the two men that there was never any official indication that Clifford disapproved of any actions taken by Cameron while he temporarily occupied the position of chief executive.[37]

Cameron's later concepts regarding such matters as indirect rule and finance were formed largely as a result of his experiences in Nigeria during this period. It has already been shown that Lugard's policy imposed an alien system, which he believed to be "traditional" rule, upon the African population. When Governor of Tanganyika, Cameron tried diligently to avoid such practices. His instructions to administrative officers in this regard were based upon the premise of shunning "as you would evil the make-believe

27

'Indirect Administration' based on nothing that is really true. It is a monster and a very dangerous one at that."[38] In recapitulating the forces that formed Cameron's attitudes toward the governing of African people, one must also note the positive influence of working as Clifford's deputy. Much later Cameron specifically stated his debt to Clifford. When thanked by members of his Secretariat for what they had learned under his tutelage, Cameron replied that "they got it but second hand from me; it all came from Hugh Clifford and their thanks are due to him and not to me."[39]

Despite Clifford's pronounced convictions on the need for major reforms in the spirit as well as the details of indirect rule, his administration accomplished very few changes in Lugard's system. One reason for this was Clifford's relative unpopularity with the Colonial Office. Any significant change he might suggest was taken as an attack upon Lugard whose reputation as the African expert had been bolstered by his position on the Mandates Commission. Nevertheless, Clifford did point out to his superiors certain shortcomings in the practical application of indirect rule in Nigeria. After his first visit to the North he informed the Colonial Office of his fundamental disagreement with the practice of allowing the emirs to rule almost unchecked over their areas. He could see the same type of static governments in northern Nigeria which he had previously experienced in Malaya. He also questioned the administration of the "pagan" Bauchi tribes which he said were being forced to accept a common form of government based upon the model of a Hausa emirate. By extension, Clifford saw this occurring in the South as well.[40] In its replies, the Colonial Office minimized Clifford's previous experience with Muslim states in Southeast Asia. His superiors dismissed his arguments about the unchanging nature of rule in the North and the poor quality of British administration elsewhere. Some saw Clifford's arguments as only reflecting his hostility to and jealousy of Lugard. A. J. Herbert in a minute paper appended to a dispatch from Clifford, accused Clifford of having gone "out to Nigeria convinced that there would be faults" and then proceeded to find them.[41]

With his superiors committed so completely to Lugard, it is not surprising that Clifford contented himself with only minimal changes in the Native Authority structure. A few provincial and district boundaries were redrawn and individual district officers were instructed to modify their attitudes toward their African charges. But Lagos was far away, and in the absence of any all-embracing policy statement indicating the scope and direction of change, the government system remained in 1925 basically what it had been five years before. Clifford, who was not insensitive to the

attitude of London, probably did not wish to wreck his
career by opposing the Colonial Office over such matters.

Lord Lugard had been deeply committed to the concept
that no true Native Authority could exist without direct
taxation. As early as 1914 he pressed the Colonial Office
to accept his plans for taxing all the southern areas. Fear-
ing African resistance in the midst of the war, Harcourt
had demurred. But in 1916 Lugard was allowed to experiment
at Oyo with a taxing system based on that of the North, and by
the time of his departure all the territory west of the Niger
River had been brought under this system. Clifford and
Cameron were able to keep direct taxation from being imposed
on the five eastern provinces. However, they did not establish different types of local government better suited to
the needs of various tribal groups. Again the temper of the
Colonial Office was largely responsible for this, as is shown
by its attitude toward the Egbas. Lugard had cooperated with
the Alake in 1914 to secure the latter's political supremacy
among the Egbas. In 1920, however, the Alake complained that
the direct tax which had been imposed by Lugard's government
was too high. Clifford agreed and argued with the Colonial
Office that the treaty of cession by which Egbaland became a
part of the British protectorate was signed without the Alake
having any detailed knowledge of what he was doing. The
direct tax paid by the Egbas was onerous in principle, and
in practice damaging to the Native Authority. Clifford wanted
to allow the Alake's government to retain as much as possible
of the central government's fifty percent share of this tax.[42]
Sir George Fiddes, the Colonial Office Permanent Undersecretary in rebutting Clifford's arguments, stated that he saw
nothing incongruous or illegal about introducing the northern
type of direct tax to the South.[43]

Pressure to extend a modified northern system of taxation to the eastern regions was successfully resisted by
Clifford's government. This had been a major objective of
the Lugard administration and the Colonial Office by the early
1920s also desired a standard taxation policy for Nigeria.[44]
However, Clifford postponed any immediate implementation of
such a policy by pointing out that the Ibo and Ibibio had
never been taxed. Instead he instructed his Secretary for
Native Affairs, S. M. Grier, to investigate and report on the
complete administrative and judicial systems of the East.
Grier's report, submitted after an exhaustive two months in-
vestigative tour of eastern Nigeria, was negative and pessimistic. He warned that the system of government imposed on
the East was alien, corrupt, and unpopular. Grier found the
consensus of European officers to be that any attempt to tax
directly the Ibo, Ijaw, and Ibibio without thoroughly reforming the political system was to invite opposition and perhaps

violent revolt.[45] Grier's report was so critical of overall
policy that his assistant, G. J. F. Tomlinson, was sent to
the East in early 1923 in order to confirm or deny the impres-
sions of his superior. Tomlinson's report was much more diplomatic and not as blunt in its criticism of the Lugard system. However, its conclusions regarding the danger of taxation and the necessity of political reform were the same.[46]

Clifford, by referring to the Grier and Tomlinson
reports, justified his position of procrastination to his
superiors. He was in no position vis à vis the Colonial
Office to launch the thoroughgoing reforms recommended by
Grier and Tomlinson. Yet on the basis of these reports he
could resist extending taxation to the East, particularly
since its imposition was not primarily to gain revenue.
When the subject of taxation once again began to agitate the
Colonial Office, Clifford assigned Sir Harry Moorhouse the
task of reinvestigating the question. Moorhouse, in August
1924, recommended that for the sake of standardization the
eastern areas be brought in line with the rest of the country.[47] Sir Hugh again avoided the issue claiming that with
the short period of time left in his term as governor it
would be unfair to his successor to do anything more. Unfortunately for Nigeria that successor, Sir Graeme Thomson,
was not such a master of the delaying action. Within a few
days of his arrival, Governor Thomson gave his approval for
taxing the five eastern provinces, thus sowing the seeds for
the women's disturbances of 1929.[48]

Even though we cannot ascertain Sir Donald's role in
the formulation of Clifford's policies, it has nevertheless
been necessary for two reasons to go into them in some detail.
The first reason is that Cameron, as Clifford's most trusted
confidant, was no doubt continually consulted on these matters by his chief. This assumption is strongly supported
when one views Cameron's actions during the three periods
he acted as governor. Thus what was done in the five-year
period of Clifford's administration becomes crucial to
understanding Cameron's predispositions when he became Governor of Tanganyika. The second and equally important reason
for viewing both the Lugard and Clifford periods in depth is
that what was done and what was left undone by them created
to a large degree the problems in Nigeria that Cameron was
called upon to resolve in 1930.

The 1920s were a crucial time for British Africa. Decisions that had been deferred during the war years finally
demanded action. In Central Africa the phasing out of the
rule of the British South Africa Company created the two new
political structures of Northern and Southern Rhodesia. All
the British territories in West Africa presented political

and economic problems similar to, if less intense than, those of Nigeria. In East Africa the most serious issue was the ultimate relationship between races. The statement of the Conservative Secretary of State for Colonies, the Duke of Devonshire, concerning "native paramountcy" was to a large extent mere rhetoric, especially in view of the large and well-organized group of white settlers in Kenya. This problem was compounded in Tanganyika by the difficulties of changing from German to British rule under the watchful eye of the League of Nations. It was under these difficult circumstances that in 1924 and 1925 the Colonial Office had to appoint new governors for most of its African territories. Sir Graeme Thomson replaced Clifford in Nigeria, William Gowers was sent to Uganda, and Sir Edward Grigg went to Kenya. In September 1924, Sir Donald Cameron was chosen to become Governor of Tanganyika.

Cameron's selection as Governor of Tanganyika was made by the short-lived first Labour government. Sir Horace Byatt was retiring as governor, and the Colonial Secretary, J. H. Thomas, wanted an extremely competent man to effect a change in Tanganyika from a semi-military to a civilian government. The new governor should ideally possess considerable administrative skills and his policies had to be in rough alignment with the objectives of the League of Nations and the attitude of the Labour government. J. H. Thomas, who admittedly knew very little of colonial affairs, nevertheless made an excellent choice when he selected his new Governor of Tanganyika.

Just how Thomas became aware of Cameron is not known. Cameron does not seem to have been a member of the Labour Party and, except for leaves of absence, he had spent over sixteen years away from Britain and its domestic problems. One must assume that Cameron's record had impressed the professionals of the Colonial Office and that his chief and friend, Sir Hugh Clifford, had recommended him highly to be governor of a territory. Cameron, in his book written over a decade after the event, mentions that the Lagos Chamber of Commerce had written petitions to the London, Manchester, and Liverpool Chambers requesting that he be appointed to succeed Clifford when the latter's term was finished in 1925.[49] Such publicity obviously helped in bringing Cameron to the attention of his superiors.

Sir Donald left Lagos for leave before taking up his new position. He was fifty-two years old and had spent sixteen years in Nigeria. All his career with the exception of one brief period had been spent in the central administration of British colonies, and he had gained a modest amount of recognition from those who appreciated such details. One

31

senior colleague underscored this when he wrote Cameron
just before he left Nigeria,

>   You will take away with you the respect and
> affection of every member of the Nigerian Secretariat.
> I have never served in an office in which the Head was so
> completely trusted and I know that every one of us will
> wish that you were not leaving Nigeria.[50]

Cameron much later noted how he felt about leaving the
place he had served so long:

>   Up to 1919 I should have left Nigeria with no
> regrets at all, but in 1924 I was very sorry to leave
> the well ordered setting of a successful administra-
> tion and a very respected chief.[51]

However, he must have seen the challenge in the new, complex
territory on the other side of Africa. In Tanganyika he would
be his own man, directly responsible for every aspect of the
reconstruction of an inefficient and confused government.
The task demanded that he rule a melange of African people
whose wide cultural and political differences made the tribal
structures of Nigeria appear simple. Tanganyika was to be
the first genuine test of Cameron's abilities as an innovator.
All else had been preparation.

3

Tanganyika Backgrounds

Sir Donald Cameron had been placed in charge of perhaps
the most challenging of all Britain's African territories.
Its governance gave full scope to talents which had lain
dormant while he remained in the shadow of Lugard and Clifford. In order to understand and appreciate fully Cameron's
achievement in Tanganyika Territory it is necessary to look
briefly at some of the complex factors that made his task so
difficult.

Tanganyika Territory had been the largest segment of
Germany's most prized African colony before World War I. It
had been a major theater of operations during the war. General Paul von Lettow-Vorbeck in the four years of conflict
had led some 3000 Europeans and 11,000 Askari in long arduous campaigns. He had forced the British to maintain large
forces in the field and expend millions of pounds trying to
defeat him. Certain parts of Tanganyika had been turned into
a wasteland by this military action, and thousands of Africans
serving with the army had died from malaria and dysentery.
Famine was also an ever present threat which had greatly reduced the population in some areas and brought the economy to
a standstill.[1] After the war thousands died in the influenza
epidemic of 1918-19.

General Jan C. Smuts, commanding the allied troops in
East Africa, managed to drive Lettow-Vorbeck's forces south
of the central railroad by the end of 1916. On 1 January
1917, Smuts instituted a civil administration over the occupied area and appointed Horace Byatt, former Lieutenant-
Governor of Malta, to head it. Byatt continued in this post
after the war ended and although Tanganyika's future was un-
certain, some form of stability and permanence of government
was given by an Order in Council of 1920. The tenuous nature
of British authority continued until July 1922 when Britian
was finally confirmed in control of the mandate by the Council of the League of Nations. All the area of the former
German territory of East Africa with the exception of Ruanda-
Urundi was placed under British jurisdiction as a class B
mandate.[2] Despite this action the boundaries of the territory were unclear. Those between the British and Belgian
mandates were not finally settled until 1935. The agreement with Portugal which delimited Tanganyika's southern

33

boundary was not concluded until 1937.[3]

Far more important for the establishment of permanent political structures was the uncertainty engendered by questions concerning the mandate itself. The key question for British administrators was where did sovereignty reside. If totally under the control of the League of Nations, then were such enabling acts as the Tanganyika Order in Council of 1920, which was closely linked to the British Foreign Jurisdiction Act, legally applicable? The Colonial Secretaries, Lord Milner and Leopold Amery, assured European settlers and investors that Tanganyika was unequivocally a part of the British Empire.[4] However, uncertainty over the territory's future undoubtedly curtailed some British investment and deterred settlers in the 1920s.

Another complication of the dual system of rule concerned rights of appeal by certain state members of the League against decisions rendered by British courts. Even more disturbing to European settlers and administrators was the possibility that the League could decide to rescind the mandate and return the territory to Germany. There were a number of influential Germans who worked hard at first to get property restored to German nationals and then later agitated for a reversion of Tanganyika to the Weimar Republic.[5] Even before Cameron's administration the British government developed a pragmatic view of the mandate where under most circumstances Tanganyika was governed as if it were a British possession. Reports were made to the Permanent Mandates Commission, but the League did not interfere with the everyday running of the territory. The League did have residual power, however, and Cameron later used this to good effect. His success after 1926 on the matter of closer union with Kenya and Uganda was partially because he threatened to disturb the ad hoc arrangement between Britian and the League and asked for a clearer definition of ultimate sovereignty.

The territory was much too large to be merely attached to a viable neighboring British protectorate such as was the case with the British mandates of Togo and the Cameroon. Discounting the condominium of the Anglo-Egyptian Sudan, Tanganyika with an area of 360,000 square miles was the second largest British protectorate in Africa. One of the world's great reservoirs of wildlife of all types and with a wide variety of terrain, Tanganyika was, nevertheless, a very poor country. The majority of the estimated 4,106,700 African population lived in small villages and practiced subsistence agriculture. There were only a few moderate sized towns, the largest being the capital, Dar es Salaam, which had a population in 1913 of only 24,000 persons.[6] There were 126 different subdivisions to the African population. Most of the people were Bantu speakers, but even the most important Bantu groups such as the Hehe, Gogo, and Shambaa had not evolved a political structure which would reflect the power their numbers would suggest. In northern Tanganyika lived the warlike, pastoral Nilo-Hamitic Masai, and in the northwest the Nilotic Bakama followed a social and economic system closely attuned to their neighbors in Ruanda-Urundi. Centered on Tabora were the large but decentralized Nyamwezi and Sukuma groups which represented a blending of Nilotic, Bantu, and Swahili. The northern coastal area was inhabited by Arabs, Swahili, and Indians, in addition to Bantu speakers. Tanganyika, while having a more diverse population than Nigeria, did not have any great, cohesive kingdoms such as the Fulani emirates or the Yoruba city-states. Also, Tanganyika was far poorer than Nigeria.

Governor Byatt's major task during both his provisional and official tenure of office was to restore order throughout the territory and improve its economy. In 1920 trade and revenue was less than half what it had been in 1914. Thus Byatt could extract little money for government use from Tanganyika itself. The hut and poll tax he instituted did not provide enough funds to cover even the rudimentary district administration. The recession in world market prices for Tanganyika's primary exports of sisal, cotton, and coffee meant that scant funds from these sources were available for recurrent expenditures let alone any new developments. Emergency loans from Britain totaling £3,135,000, and £403,000 in outright grants were necessary to enable the Tanganyika government to continue operations.[7] After 1924 when exports reached a total of £2.6 million, the economic position steadily improved, thus enabling Cameron to devote a larger portion of his time to political and social matters than was possible for his predecessor.

Sir Horace's government applied what surplus funds were available to improving services at the major ports and making the railways fully operative again. The latter task was not completed until 1924. Attempts to improve the quantity and quality of agricultural products generally proved unsuccessful. This was certainly the case of the government attempt to start a rubber industry which failed through lack of funds. Potentially the most economically viable section of the Tanganyika population were the European settlers. Slightly over 2400 in number, they were concentrated in the north near Moshi and Arusha. Of this number, less than 1600 were British subjects. Most of the settlers were relative newcomers from Britain, Kenya, or South Africa who had bought their lands very cheaply at the sales of ex-enemy property. There were still a considerable number of German residents, although Byatt had greatly restricted their

immigration and residence by an ordinance in 1923.[8] The
white settlers tended to overestimate their immediate economic importance since in the early 1920s they provided only
a small portion of Tanganyika's exports. Due to their real
and imagined affinities to their neighbors in Kenya, they
wished, as far as possible, to have Kenya's land and economic
policies duplicated in Tanganyika. Their attitudes, in combination with those of colonial administrators in Whitehall
and Nairobi, in a few years created a major crisis for Tanganyika and presented Sir Donald his most difficult problem.

     Governor Byatt had been handicapped by a small, inex-
perienced administrative staff. At the beginning of his administration he had to depend upon personnel loaned by the
Union of South Africa and other governments of East and Central Africa. Many of his administrators had until recently
been military officers serving with the forces in East Africa.
The staff bequeathed to Cameron in 1925 was still small in
numbers, but was as well trained and experienced as any in
British Africa. Given the facts of inadequate staff and
little money, it was not surprising that Byatt changed only
slightly the system of administration he inherited from the
Germans.

     German occupation of East Africa had been far more
violent than its British counterpart in Kenya or even Uganda.
The Hehe resisted the Germans from 1891 to 1897, and Hasan
bin Omari led a revolt in the Kilwa area which lasted until
1895. The Germans had to send military expeditions to sub-
due the Chagga, the Nyamwezi, the Makonde, and the Ngoni in
the years just before the turn of the century. The most
serious resistance to German occupation, however, was the
so-called Maji-Maji rebellion of 1905-07 which was at first
centered on the Kilwa district. It later spread to the
majority of the peoples south of the Rufiji River who detested
the Akida system of rule and resented forced labor and the
hut tax. The rebels received approval from their tribal
religious leaders and the revolt became a near national movement whose objective was the expulsion of the Europeans. In
order to quell the two-year uprising, the Germans after 1905
used the full complement of modern weapons against the rebels
and employed scorched earth tactics throughout the southern
region. In this struggle over 75,000 Africans lost their
lives, the whole south-eastern section of Tanganyika was
devastated, and the indigenous traditional society of the
dissidents was almost totally destroyed.[9] It is against
this background of German military pacification and authori-
tarian control that one must assess the political system
devised by the Germans and passed on to the British.

     In three large areas of their empire--Ruanda, Urundi,
and Bukoba--the Germans appointed Residents. These Residents,
although exercising ultimate control, were generally content

to allow traditional rulers to exercise a great amount of
authority. After World War I, only the Bukoba area was included in the British mandate of Tanganyika, Ruanda and
Urundi passing to Belgium. In the rest of German East Africa,
the Germans had considered tribal authority to be too weak
to allow for the Resident system. They therefore retained to
a large degree the type of rule that had been evolved by the
coastal Arabs. Tanganyika was divided into twenty-two districts and these were placed under direct German rule. The
Germans did not attempt to draw district boundaries to accommodate the different peoples living there. Thus a boundary
could divide a whole people while at the same time bringing
together traditional enemies under the same local political
organization. Civilian, and in a few cases military, officers
were appointed as district administrators (<u>Bezirksamtmann</u>) of
these arbitrary subdivisions. Each was responsible to the
governor for maintenance of law and order in his district as
well as for the collection of taxes. Districts were subdivided into groups of villages where the total population
was approximately 25,000 persons. A native official, in
many cases an Arab or Swahili, called an Akida was placed in
charge of these subdivisions. He was given certain magis-
terial powers and was made responsible for law and order in
his area. A further division of authority occurred by placing each village under the charge of a headman called a
Jumbe. The chances of the Jumbe's being a part of the traditional system was greater than in the case of the Akida's.
Nevertheless, their exercise of autocratic power was generally alien to the African concept of counselor government.
In some very important districts or cities there was a higher
official called a Liwale (a Swahili term meaning governor)
who was appointed by the German administration to supervise
the activities of the Akidas in the district.[10] There is
considerable evidence that the system was despised by a
majority of the Africans even before World War I.

Aside from its attitude toward traditional rule, the
major weakness of the German system which was carried over
during the early years of British rule was the shortage of
qualified European personnel. In 1914 there were fewer than
eighty German administrators for the entire territory.
Therefore they could not, even had they wished to, exercise
adequate control of the Akidas and Jumbes. The actual power
in almost all areas was exercised by these subordinate
African appointees. Many of the Akidas were dedicated, competent officers, but the system was ready-made for corruption
and abuse of authority. At the onset of the mandate the
British retained intact the twenty-two districts established
by the Germans and, with minor modifications, the Akida system.

German ordinances and regulations remained in effect unless they were in open conflict with British law. Even the same Akidas and Jumbes were retained in office if they had not overtly displayed anti-British feelings. The Kwanja's or plot tenancy for land occupation introduced by the Germans in 1905 was retained by Governor Byatt even after the issuance of the comprehensive land ordinances of 1923 and 1924. Tanganyika's taxing system remained basically the same, with villagers being required to pay direct taxes as well as rendering services to their local rulers.[11]

The major changes in the local government system under Byatt were introduced by the Native Authority Ordinances of 1921 and 1923 which legalized chiefs or traditional rulers, defined their authority, and laid the groundwork for Cameron's more extensive reforms.[12] The ordinances thus checked the erosion of the chiefs' authority in many areas of Tanganyika. Traditional rulers, where they could be easily discovered by the district commissioners, replaced the Akida and Jumbe system. In many other areas where the Akida system was retained, the Akidas' authority was modified, thus restricting their near autocratic powers. The East African Commission Report of 1924-25 applauded these efforts by Governor Byatt and concluded that there still existed throughout much of Tanganyika the rudiments of traditional African government.[13] Nevertheless, the governor had ordered no systematic survey of African systems of rule in Tanganyika. What had been developed by the end of his term of office was a composite of the German system and an embryo type of indirect rule. District commissioners in almost every locale tended to use the African leaders, whether traditional or not, as mouthpieces of the administration. The Africans were, in effect, nothing more than agents of a peculiar system of direct rule. Cameron remarked that the government before his arrival "seems to have had a somewhat vague and undefined bias towards administering the people (through their Chiefs) as it was sometimes loosely described, but it was not much more than dumb aspiration to which no real effect had been given for the time being."[14] There were chiefs called "Sultans," but they had no properly constituted courts of their own, except in Bukoba. There was also no significant local revenue so there was no pressing need for Native Treasuries.

It appears that the small British field staff had ambivalent feelings toward Governor Byatt. They disliked his authoritarianism and many district officers were irked by his obvious ineptitude when dealing with certain specific local problems. However, because of his lack of knowledge of local government and the many more pressing problems demanding his attention, Byatt did not try to impose standardized

central control over district administrations. This <u>ad</u> <u>hoc</u>
system left individual officers great freedom to decide for
themselves their relationships with their African charges.

By 1924 it was apparent to many senior administrative
officers that a major reorganization of local government
would have to be undertaken. In October, after the departure
of Governor Byatt, they received permission from the acting
governor to hold a meeting at Dar es Salaam to consider
recommendations for changing the system. The major problem
discussed at the meeting was the type of organizational structure needed for the territory. The officers unanimously
agreed upon the need to create a provincial administration
intermediate between the governor and the district commissioners. They envisioned the provincial commissioners as having
a great amount of autonomy from control by the central government. They also urged the creation of the post of Secretary
for Native Affairs to insure better liaison between officers
in the field and the central administration. The senior
staff also wanted the central government to rebate to the
districts larger amounts from tax funds. They suggested that
these funds should be expended by newly created district
Native Treasuries.[15] The acting governor, Sir John Scott,
disagreed with some of the proposals, particularly those
concerning local government which he thought would give too
much independence to native rulers. But even had Sir John
been in total agreement with the suggestions of his subordinates, it would have been unusual for the Colonial Office
to sanction such a major change as that proposed before the
arrival of the new governor. The most important thing accomplished by the Dar es Salaam meeting was that the senior
officers of Tanganyika had collectively informed the home
government of the need for general government reform. Cameron's task was thus made considerably easier since he did not
have to convince his superiors of the need for change, but
only of the form and direction it should take.

By the mid-1920s British official attitudes toward Tanganyika were being tested by two conflicting philosophies.
One was that so forcefully enunciated by Lord Delamere, the
pioneer settler of Kenya. He saw in the highlands of East
Africa a place well suited for European colonization. Delamere had worked for a quarter of a century attempting to convince different governments to give their support to colonization ventures. By the mid-1920s he was the spokesman for
a small but extremely powerful group of persons in England,
Kenya, and Tanganyika who placed the interests of the minority white community above those of the African majority as
well as the small Indian community.[16] From 1918 to 1923
this group had attempted to restrict the privileges of
Indian residents in Kenya while at the same time assuring

responsible government for Europeans. It failed in both
attempts. The Duke of Devonshire's white paper, which stated
that the well-being of the African population was the paramount concern of the British government, effectively blocked
the white settlers' schemes for responsible government.[17]
Although Britain's later actions in Kenya were not directed
toward native paramountcy, Devonshire's pronouncement in 1923
was in keeping with the highest aspirations of British rule
in Africa as well as the guiding philosophy of the League of
Nations.

The other set of attitudes toward East Africa was perhaps
best exemplified in Article 22 of the Covenant of the League.
In that article the rationale for the mandates was that a
mandatory power should control the affairs of a mandate until
the people of the territory were able to govern themselves.
For the mandating power this implied not only the role of
protector, but also of educator. Britain had accepted the
responsibility of expending its time, effort, and money on
a "civilizing" mission which would bring the people of Tanganyika to the point of self-determination as soon as possible. Some of the terms of the Tanganyika mandate were very
specific. Britain was "to promote to the utmost the material
and moral well-being and the social progress of . . . Tanganyika's inhabitants." Further it was to "respect the rights
and safeguard the interests of the native population" in
framing laws related to land. Britain was enjoined to protect Africans from abuse and fraud by carefully supervising
labor contracts and the recruitment of labor.[18] The British
government was required to make annual reports to the League
to justify its conduct and to allow League officials to in-
spect the activities of the Tanganyika government.

It is important to stress here that a governor of Tanganyika had to satisfy two masters. Even though the League's
presence was not obvious, the fact that it retained ultimate
sovereignty made it a factor no governor could ignore. As
long as the Colonial Office was in agreement with the League,
as had been the case during Byatt's tenure, then there were
no problems. However, Sir Donald Cameron early in his term
of office was presented with a new dilemma since the Conservative Secretary of State, Leopold S. Amery, was on many
issues in substantial agreement with Lord Delamere and the
European settlers. Aside from Amery's personal predilictions,
there was the possibility of closer union between the three
East African territories which would allow for substantial
savings to the British taxpayer.[19]

The question of closer union with all its potential
ramifications for the African community became the major
problem of Cameron's term as governor and it eventually
caused him to resist the wishes of his superiors in London.

Therefore one should look briefly at its development before Cameron arrived. The chief advocates of closer union had been the white settlers of the Kenya highlands. Their spokesman, Lord Delamere, had invested over twenty-five years of work and his entire fortune in pursuance of the concept of a European colony in East Africa. The settlers had received considerable support for the great white state from such important British officials as Leopold Amery and Winston Churchill,[20] although they had been unsuccessful in gaining official adherence to the policy of white supremacy in the Kenya territory. However, despite the pious statement of paramountcy contained in the Devonshire declaration, the British government still remained pro-settler, and the small Indian population was checked in its ambitions for equality.

Lord Delamere proposed a dual policy similar to that which would later be recommended by Lugard in the Dual Mandate as the only solution to East Africa's problems. While assuring economically strong colonies for Britain, such a policy would ultimately benefit the African. Delamere believed that the only way for civilization to prosper in Africa would be for the African to attach himself firmly to those representatives of a higher culture, and he argued persuasively that any other procedure would result in dire harm to both black and white communities. At one juncture he eloquently declaimed that, "In the case of the native peoples, their progress must depend on the fact that the lamp of civilization is kept burning brightly before them."[21]

The British settlers in northern Tanganyika tended to agree with Delamere and their counterparts in Kenya. For a long while they had felt insecure in possession of their land because of doubts as to the ultimate future of Tanganyika. They had just begun by 1925 to believe assurances from London that Tanganyika would remain British, when certain influential Germans showed a zealous revival of interest in regaining Tanganyika and German farmers were once more allowed to settle there. The farmers in the vicinity of Arusha and Moshi were also afraid of economic competition from the Chagga people who were beginning to plant coffee. They feared the quality of coffee exported from Tanganyika would suffer and the price paid for all Tanganyika coffee would be lowered. The white farmers claimed they needed a more tractible, larger labor force and they wanted more stringent labor laws which would force more Africans to take up work on the farms of Europeans. They believed that many of their objectives could be achieved if the government in Dar es Salaam would pattern itself on its neighbor to the north.

The agitation of the Kenyan Indian community for equal treatment with Europeans in the years immediately after World

War I caused concerted humanitarian opposition to develop in
Britain against the supremacist attitudes of the white settlers. As early as December 1920 the opponents of white
supremacy had petitioned the Colonial Office for a commission
to inquire into the guiding principles of imperial policy in
East Africa. The publication of the 1923 White Paper caused
both the humanitarians' and Delamere's adherents to press
for such a commission. In April 1924 a parliamentary motion
for such a commission was adopted and the Labour government
appointed a three man commission comprising Major A. G. Church,
F. C. Linfield, M. P., with W. G. A. Ormsby-Gore (later Lord
Harlech) as its chairman. The commission was instructed to
inquire into steps necessary to secure close policy coordina-
tion of the three territories and also ways in which the lives
of Africans could be improved. Even though the Conservatives
returned to power in November, there is no evidence that they
attempted to prejudice the findings of the commission.

Before arriving in Kenya, Ormsby-Gore had tended to
support the humanitarians in their charges that the land and
labor policies in East Africa were detrimental to the well-
being of the African. During his stay in East Africa he
modified his viewpoint. While in Kenya he and the two other
commissioners were chauffeured from place to place by white
settlers, usually in Lord Delamere's yellow Packard.[22] It
was, therefore, not unusual that the commission members saw
only what their European guides wished them to see. Also,
there were few Africans or Indians who could present their
case with such lucidity as Delamere. In the same month that
Cameron arrived in Tanganyika to take up his new post, the
commission submitted its two hundred page report to the Secretary of State. To the qualified gratification of Amery
and his supporters, the report, although negating immediate
political union, did suggest eventual closer union and the
implementation of the dual policy wherever possible.[23] The
Ormsby-Gore report, while recognizing that the two factors
of distance and lack of funds prevented the immediate implementation of closer union, nevertheless recommended it as a
future goal. It suggested periodic meetings of the governors
of the territories concerned in order to discuss common
problems. With such consultation, ways of achieving greater
efficiency in administration could possibly be found and the
necessary foundation laid for eventual political union. The
report, while representing a reversal of Ormsby-Gore's previous position, did not go far enough to please Amery, who
apparently was committed to closer union even before he
succeeded J. H. Thomas as Colonial Secretary.

Leopold Amery had more legislative and administrative
experience in colonial affairs than most of his predecessors.
He was fifty years of age when the Conservatives were returned

to power in November 1924. He had been well educated at
Harrow and Balliol College, Oxford, and had served as a
Times correspondent during the Boer War and later helped
compile the mammoth seven volume Times history of that conflict. A member of Parliament after 1911, he had served as
Assistant Secretary to the War Cabinet, had been at Versail-
les on the staff of the Secretary of State for War, and had
been Parliamentary Undersecretary of State for the Colonies
during Lord Milner's two-year term after 1919. From 1922 to
1924 he had served as First Lord of the Admiralty.[24] Amery
was an able administrator and a very powerful figure in the
Conservative Party, and he had decided negative opinions on
the stated Devonshire policy. In this he concurred with the
mercurial but powerful Winston Churchill who previously as
Secretary of State for the Colonies had done everything in
his power to insure the triumph of white settlement. From
Amery's replies to embarrassing questions addressed to him
in the House of Commons by humanitarians, it became apparent
that he had no intention of applying the doctrine of native
paramountcy in Kenya. But, although deeply committed to
closer union, he could not ignore the Ormsby-Gore report and
proceed on his own volition to unify the territories. A
prime example of the restriction on his freedom of action
concerned the appointment of the new Governor of Kenya.
Amery had to turn down Lord Lloyd, his first choice for the
position, since Lloyd had made a condition of his appointment
his almost immediate assignment as the governor-general of
all three territories.[25] Instead Amery appointed Sir Edward
Grigg to the post to act as his chief agent in bringing about
the desired goal of union.

Grigg's background was very similar to that of Amery.
He had been educated at an English public school and at Oxford, and had worked for a decade after 1903 on the editorial
staff of the Times. When the war began he joined the Grena-
dier Guards, eventually obtaining the rank of lieutenant-
colonel. Later he became the military secretary to the Prince
of Wales and accompanied the future King Edward VII on his
visits to Canada, Australia, and New Zealand. In 1921 he
became the private secretary to the Prime Minister, David
Lloyd George, and in the following year he was elected to the
House of Commons. Grigg had become accustomed to close
association with some of the most important men in England.
Reading his reminiscences written much later, one can savor
the pleasure he felt at being called to a private audience
with the King before going out to Kenya.[26] Grigg was proud
that Lord Milner, among other powerful men, had urged his
appointment as Governor of Kenya upon Prime Minister Baldwin.
Sir Edward was a handsome man, self-assured, with one major

43

defect--excessive pride. Most of his administrative experience had been in relationship with men who exercised near
absolute power. In Kenya, his own master for the first time,
he reveled in the pomp and ceremony of his office. Grigg had
been given a mission by those in England whom he admired
and, like the good soldier he was, he planned to overcome all
petty objections to closer union.

The Governor of Uganda, Sir William Gowers, played a
minor role in the controversy which developed later between
Sir Donald Cameron and the protagonists of closer union.
Appointed Governor of Uganda in 1925, Gowers had served in
Nigeria with Cameron where he had been acting lieutenant-
governor of the southern provinces and also Lagos Colony
Administrator. This earlier close association had not en-
deared the two men to one another. Their mutual dislike was
similar to the earlier antipathy between the governors of the
Gold Coast and Nigeria, Guggisberg and Clifford. Differences
between the peoples and economies of Tanganyika and Uganda
were obviously important determiners of the philosophies of
government held by Cameron and Gowers. However, their feelings toward each other guaranteed the heightening of any disagreements between them. In all the Governors' Conferences,
Gowers was a willing if somewhat silent ally of those who
wanted closer union, and could be relied upon to support most
of Grigg's proposals.

Sir Donald Cameron at the time of his appointment as
governor in 1925 was imperfectly aware of the importance
attached by so many powerful men to some kind of political
union of the East African territories. Amery had never informed him that he considered Grigg his chief agent in East
Africa to secure closer union, and throughout the early phase
of the controversy, Cameron believed that the pressure for
this course of action came entirely from Grigg acting as the
spokesman for resident European interests. Cameron's early
dislike for Grigg as a pushy amateur was based on his misap-
prehension.[27] Acting upon Colonial Office instructions,
Grigg called for a Governors' Conference to convene at
Nairobi in January 1926. The conference and its aftermath
presented Cameron with a choice. To oppose those who supported closer union could jeopardize his career without necessarily securing any modification of the suggestions implicit
in the Ormsby-Gore report. The most obvious course of action
for Cameron would have been to concur in the decisions of
his superiors and cooperate fully with the Colonial Secretary
and the Governor of Kenya. But Cameron, finally in charge of
his own territory, brilliant, stubborn, and committed to justice for the African, chose instead to work against closer
union. His campaign against its implementation was correlate
with and just as important a milestone as his more publicized
reform of Tanganyika's native administration.

4

The Closer Union Controversy

Sir Donald Cameron arrived in East Africa in April 1925 before either of his East African counterparts, Sir Edward Grigg or Sir William Gowers, and immediately set about the task of educating himself in the intricacies of managing the huge Tanganyika Territory. Cameron very quickly approved in principle most of the suggestions made by the Conference of Senior Civil Servants which had been held in Dar es Salaam the year before. He very early established the habit of traveling throughout Tanganyika trying to acquaint himself first hand with the major problems of the rural Africans. Cameron had two reasons for these long, tiring journeys. One was his desire to learn the reactions of the men in the field to his sweeping reforms, and the second was to have the young officers see him in person and not as some unapproachable autocrat located hundreds of miles away, who would put into effect startling changes without consultation. In November 1925 he undertook his first safari to the north to meet representatives of the European settlers at Moshi and Arusha.[1] Although he did not expect and did not effect a reconciliation with the settlers, he gave them a chance to air their opinions directly to him. Other safaris were made specifically to communicate directly with African leaders. During these meetings with traditional rulers he appeared in full dress uniform complete with the gold braid, cocked hat, and feathers of a governor. Sir Edward Grigg, a much more martial figure than Cameron, could never understand this and presumably dismissed it as play acting. But Cameron knew that his visits and the attendant ceremonies pleased the traditional rulers, supported their authority, and forwarded the implementation of his ideas of indirect rule. Wearing a formal uniform in hot weather was little enough to pay for any modicum of success in this direction.

Sir Donald made a number of decisions not connected with local government soon after coming to Tanganyika. A minor but important change concerned bringing Tanganyika within a standard time system. On his arrival in Dar es Salaam he asked the time and discovered that the only acceptable time in Tanganyika was the clock in the former Lutheran Church at Dar es Salaam. This time could apparently be changed at the whim of either the Postmaster General or the Director of Public Works. The following morning Cameron prompty ordered that Tanganyika accept zonal time.[2] This important change, small within itself, was an example of how quickly Cameron arrived at his solution to a given problem.

A further example of how quickly the new governor showed that he intended to be a mover and shaker even in small things concerned flogging as a punishment for offenses in the King's African Rifles. Shortly after coming to Tanganyika, Cameron had witnessed the whipping of a drummer boy as punishment for a very minor infraction. Officers of the military unit informed him that if whipping were abolished, discipline among the ranks would be very hard to maintain. Sir Donald agreed not to abolish whipping, but demanded that before any such punishment was carried out in the future he be provided with papers setting out the full details of the charge, the defense, and the presiding officer's opinion. Cameron knew the positive value of bureaucratic detail. Faced with the need for considerable extra paperwork, the practice of indiscriminate whipping was stopped and the entire practice abolished in 1928.[3]

The field of transport and communications gave Cameron another opportunity to test his vision against the advice of his more conservative experts. He decided in 1928 that the various types of mechanical transport available were far enough advanced for supplies to be moved to any part of the territory without the use of head porterage. Despite dire predictions of what would happen in some of the more remote areas, Cameron decided to abolish head porterage. There was no noticeable change in the quality of the supply service throughout Tanganyika after this order had been effected.

Once Cameron had decided upon a particular action, it was nearly impossible to dissuade him from its immediate implementation. A good example of this self-confidence is seen in his insistence upon creating a Legislative Council. The Governor of Tanganyika was even more of an autocrat in theory than governors in most other British territories, since his complete authority was unchecked by the Executive Council which was composed entirely of official members. Undoubtedly Cameron's position toward a Legislative Council was conditioned by his remembrance of some of the problems Clifford had inherited in Nigeria because Lugard had not evolved a council which could act as a proper sounding board for proposed legislation. Cameron was determined that the major reforms he contemplated in the Tanganyika system would be scrutinized by a Legislative Council. Against the advice of his Chief Secretary, Sir John Scott, Cameron early in his tenure as governor pressed his ideas on the Colonial Office. His proposals were eventually accepted, and a twenty-three man Legislative Council was approved in 1926.[4] Cameron very soon showed his pragmatic approach in filling seven of the ten unofficial positions on the council. He was no democrat and, despite his affection for the African, refused to appoint any to the council. He explained this to the Legislative Council by stating, "The native community cannot be represented because for the present a native cannot be found with sufficient command of the English language to take part in the debates of the Council."[5] His decision against immediately appointing an African to the council was reinforced by his suspicions of educated Africans. Still in the process of creating his Native Authority system, Sir Donald did not want to appoint any African to the Legislative Council who would not be able to speak for a significant number of Africans. As far as Cameron was concerned, only a traditional ruler could do this.

One of the governor's early schemes to arouse public interest in the proceedings of the newly formed Legislative Council was to have it hold a session in the district with the largest white population. Cameron had visited the north in November 1925 and was aware of the dissatisfaction of the plantation owners with government actions. He therefore decided to have the Legislative Council meet at Arusha, the northern provincial headquarters. G. F. Sayers, clerk of the council, remembered much later that,

> Cameron insisted that the surroundings should be worthy of the occasion. The whole furniture of the Council Chamber was moved by boat and train to Arusha, and proceedings opened with a guard of honour, with ceremony and uniforms attracting a large crowd of local Europeans. But alas, interest was short lived and attendance quickly diminished until only two or three ladies turned up--to knit! while the Council busied itself with legislation.[6]

Perhaps this lack of visible support from the white settlers for the new instrument of government helped convince Cameron of the shallowness of their commitment to Tanganyika's future.

The governor, late in 1925, was studying the feasibility of launching two major development projects. One was the improvement of the harbor facilities at Dar es Salaam. Increasing prosperity of the territory had already indicated the inadequacies of the port. Cameron gave his assent to the detailed plans early in 1926, and soon after the Colonial Office concurred in that decision.[7] Much more controversial was the plan to build an extension of the main railway to the port of Mwanza on Lake Victoria. Cameron and his advisors believed that such a spur line would benefit central and northwestern Tanganyika by linking these areas to new markets.

47

Lord Delamere and most of the white settlers of East Africa opposed the project claiming that it would damage the revenues of the Uganda-Kenya line. They argued that the export crops from northwest Tanganyika could use either road or lake transport and that the railroad was an unnecessary expenditure. Cameron eventually rejected such arguments as having little foundation. The actions of the delegates at the first Governors' Conference in condemning the Mwanza extension was another confirmation to Cameron that his fellow governors were unable to view any question on the basis of its merits. Cameron persisted in his decision to go ahead with the construction, and in April 1926, the Colonial Office gave its approval for the Mwanza line.[8]

Cameron had begun the reorganization of the central Secretariat in 1925 which culminated the next year in the regrading of most of the European and African staff.[9] He had also started the selection process to get the best available men in the right places in the Secretariat, a procedure he understood so well. The example the governor gave to his staff was one of concentration and dedication. He did not have a private secretary per se, although some of that work was done by an old classmate from Rathmines school, Captain Smith. The testimony of many who served under Cameron is that Smith was not very efficient and was tolerated by Cameron for the sake of old times. Cameron did his own typing and used to work far into the night, often to the discomfiture of younger staff members. It has been mentioned before that Sir Donald was an "all-rounder" with considerable knowledge of almost every facet of administration from local government to finance. To this was added his ability to scan lengthy, complex reports and to abstract very quickly their most salient points. One of his junior officers in the Secretariat recalled thirty-five years later an incident which is indicative of Cameron's ability:

> I well remember an occasion when a despatch had to be written on the re-organization of the King's African Rifles--and as everyone seemed a bit shy about doing it he said he would do it himself. So he sat down to a typewriter and typed about a dozen foolscap pages (full of facts and figures) with one finger--and at the end of the day there were practically no alterations except his own minor ones. It was an amazing performance.[10]

His department heads soon came to understand that their work had to be done accurately and that they had to know all facets of a given problem. It was not long before the governor had impressed his stamp of excellence upon those who worked in Dar es Salaam.

One of the early reforms of the central administration was the creation of the position of Secretary for Native Affairs. This had been one of the main recommendations of the 1924 conference of Tanganyika senior civil servants. Although Cameron's view of the role of provincial officers differed substantially from those of his field staff, he saw at once the necessity to have an official who would be directly responsible for coordinating local government policy throughout Tanganyika. The Secretary for Native Affairs could become one of the key positions whereby the central authority could impose itself upon the chaotic organization of the territory. Cameron appointed Charles Dundas who had considerable field experience, particularly in the Mt. Kilamanjaro area, to fill this post. Dundas and his assistant, Philip Mitchell, were immediately put to work superintending the collection of data on the various African peoples of Tanganyika as a preliminary to the establishment of Cameron's Native Authority system.[11]

It is clear that Cameron himself was extremely busy throughout most of 1925 with an enormous number of problems. In addition to those already mentioned, he was spending a great amount of time on the total reorganization of local administration throughout Tanganyika and the writing of the political memoranda which were to guide these changes. Thus it is understandable that he viewed the convening of the first Governor's Conference at Nairobi with something less than enthusiasm.

The conference, which had first been suggested by the Ormsby-Gore report, convened in Nairobi on 26 January 1926, and proved to be the first round of a struggle that outlasted Cameron's tenure as governor. Sir Edward Grigg, who believed he had a mandate from the highest authorities to work for the union of British dependencies in East and Central Africa, presided over the conference. Grigg was in his element as the chairman and host of the conference, and he was certain that there would be little difficulty in obtaining a consensus upon many of the major points that would be discussed. This first conference was attended by the governors of Kenya, Uganda, Tanganyika, Nyasaland, and Northern Rhodesia, and their staffs. The Resident of Zanzibar was also present. The conference began with a long, fulsome address by Grigg, followed by shorter ones from the other representatives. Cameron's speech was a model of brevity. He did not commit himself to anything except to work for the success of the conference. After a few amenities, he closed by saying that there was a full agenda to be considered, time was circumscribed, so he suggested the delegates should get to work.[12]

Cameron spent less than two weeks at the conference, leaving on 8 February before the conference closed. Thus his later statement that he was relieved "when it [the conference] had finished its ponderous labours and I could get back to my work" was not strictly true.[13] He had very early decided that the meeting was a mistake and left as soon as he could without being openly discourteous. Most of the other governors had been in their posts less time than he, they took themselves too seriously, and most were prepared to run roughshod over any negative opinion.

One of the most important problems common to all the territories was that related to labor, and there was considerable pressure to develop a common labor policy. Grigg, knowing he had solid support from the white community, pressed for a standard law which could be used to coerce the Africans to take up employment on the white farms. Such a proposal was at variance with Cameron's principles against forcing Africans to work against their will. He noted that European employers in Tanganyika who maintained good standards of wages, housing, and food had no trouble getting Africans to work for them. He believed that "coercion of labour by pressure of direct taxation is little, if anything, removed from the direct coercion of labour; the latter is the more honest course."[14] Of the attitude exemplified by the Governor's Conference, Cameron wrote, "There was to me something unreal in the whole proceedings, and when at an early stage, one of the members moved that a labour law of certain character should be introduced in each of the Territories I thought I was in the middle ages."[15]

In this connection it should be noted that Cameron's labor policies were quite advanced and very successful. In 1926, Cameron accepted the major recommendations of a Special Labour Commissioner and created a Labour Department.[16] This department, with a commissioner, four assistants, and subordinate staff, had its headquarters in Morogoro. Labor officers were permanently stationed in the plantation areas of the north, and labor camps were established to accommodate laborers traveling to and from the plantations. By 1930 there were seven well-organized camps operating which handled over 70,000 workers for the plantations. The Labour Department, in addition to supervising labor contracts and helping provide an adequate labor supply for the plantations, was also responsible for inspecting labor conditions on public undertakings and the railways. Cameron remarked that the department was "most efficient" and that it pleased him that "the interests of employees and the employers were being supervised by a competent body of officers at a critical time in the country's economic history."[17] Unfortunately, because of the depression, the department was abolished soon after

50

Cameron left Tanganyika and was not reestablished until 1938.

Correlate with the discussion of labor at the 1926 Governors' Conference was the pressure for a common land policy for all the British East African territories. Here again most of the delegates tended to be greatly influenced by Grigg's reflections of the Kenyan settlers' views on land alienation and Native Reserves. Cameron agreed with the desire to bring more land under cultivation, develop a better export potential, and protect the land from abuse. He even agreed with the stated generalizations concerning the desirability of encouraging settlement by Europeans and the need for a ready supply of African labor. However, he made two reservations which were totally at variance with the policy of Kenya. They were,

> (A) The land policy of the Territory Tanganyika as defined in the Land Ordinance whereunder the land is vested in the Governor for the use and common benefit, direct or indirect of the natives, to remain unimpaired in every respect; (B) The Government of Tanganyika does not commit itself to the policy of Native Reserves, to which it is opposed.[18]

In retrospect it is difficult to understand why the governors were not satisfied at the first conference with merely exploring those common problems where there was considerable agreement. Instead they proceeded to act as if the conference were a legislative body which somehow had been endowed with powers of interference in the affairs of an individual territory. Presumably the majority of those present at Nairobi believed that their decisions would be accepted without demur by the Colonial Office which would then order a reluctant governor to abide by the will of the majority.

The conference approved the principle of labor legislation that would provide white settlers with a more regular supply of workers. The presumption seemed to be that the new laws should follow closely the Kenya model where taxation was used as a lever to force Africans to work for Europeans. Much was also said about the need to encourage more colonization and to guarantee certain suitable areas of Africa for white settlement. Complementing discussion of these subjects was the expressed fear of some of the delegates that Africans would be encouraged to begin certain kinds of agricultural activity which would be detrimental to the white farmers. In this connection a majority of the governors concurred with a resolution which asked Cameron to stop the Chagga from cultivating coffee.[19] This suggestion was ignored by Cameron, as were most of the other resolutions of the conference.

Tanganyika seemed to be considered the territory most out of step with what the assembled governors believed to be good. Cameron's decision to go ahead with the construction of the railway spur to Mwanza was questioned, and a resolution to this effect was passed by the conference, with only Cameron registering his dissent. Another subject that engendered much discussion was the boundary between Tanganyika and Kenya which divided the Masai territory. Grigg expressed himself at length on the need to remove this barrier and allow for one set of government directives to be given for all the Masai.[20]

It is impossible today to know exactly what Grigg's feelings were at the close of the conference. He must have been vaguely troubled by some of Cameron's statements. But he had managed the conference well, most of the governors had supported him on crucial issues, and he did know that the Colonial Secretary wanted standardization in East Africa based as far as possible on the Kenya model. Grigg may even have been encouraged by the fact that Cameron had said very little on some of the controversial points. If this were so, it showed how little he understood the way in which the Governor of Tanganyika operated.

Beginning in February, 1926, Sir Donald sent a series of dispatches to his superiors in London in which he revealed the weakness of Grigg's position and at the same time subtly showed his own opposition to Amery's and Grigg's concept of closer union. Cameron informed the Colonial Office that he had not stated his views publicly since he wanted to ascertain the views of the Colonial Secretary before engaging in debate with the other governors. He made it clear that he did not oppose European settlement per se, and he wrote that he had no arguments with which he could publicly defend a completely anti-colonial attitude. Furthermore, European farmers were an obvious economic benefit to Tanganyika. Cameron argued, however, that colonization could be carried out only where the area was suitable for European settlement and where it could be done "without depriving the native population of sufficient land for its own use." In the long dispatch of 25 February paraphrasing the Devonshire declaration, Cameron wrote, "It is not, I think necessary for me to affirm again that the interests of the native should be paramount."[21] This was not exactly what was intended by many of the supporters of European settlement who had never agreed with the concept of native paramountcy in East Africa. Instead they would have echoed Lord Cranworth, Chairman of the Advisory Committee of the Trade and Information Office, who in a speech concerning East Africa delivered in April pronounced, "One stipulation must be postulated. Never must the interests of the white population be allowed to be swamped

52

by the interests of the native, however numerous."[22]

Cameron also pointed out to his superiors the ambiguities of previous Colonial Office statements concerning the acquisition of land in Tanganyika by Europeans. Winston Churchill, for example, for all his support of the settlers, had stated in a dispatch in 1922 that "acquisition by non-natives of plantation or pastoral areas should be limited and exceptional while the granting of large 'concessions' will be impossible."[23] Cameron commented that exactly what this meant in concrete terms escaped him. Colonial Office personnel could not see that at this juncture Cameron was asking them to give him more specific guidance. Charles Strachey, one of the senior Colonial Office administrators, minuted to Sir Samuel Wilson on 3 May that he thought Cameron was just being difficult since the vagueness of the term "exceptional" should not have disturbed anyone so long as the bulk of the land remained in native hands. However, Strachey did agree with another of Cameron's arguments against encouraging more settler emigration. In view of Tanganyika's special position as a mandate, preference could not be given to British subjects in any large-scale colonization project. The British government did not want to see large areas of Tanganyika revert to German ownership as was being seriously suggested by some influential Germans such as the financier, Dr. Hjalmar Schacht. Strachey could see that it was not to Britain's advantage "to spend millions on a railway . . . in order to enable compact settlement of German population to send colonial raw materials to Germany on a cheap rate."[24]

Another telling point made by Cameron in his dispatches was the extra-legal nature of the Governors' Conference. He criticized the assumption that the decisions of the conference had any binding force upon Tanganyika. At best it could be considered only a consultative body whose suggestions could be accepted or rejected by a governor. Cameron also questioned the wisdom of having decisions of a purely domestic nature such as the Mwanza railway put to a vote by representatives of other territories. How much, he asked, could the Governor of Northern Rhodesia know about the problems of Tanganyika.[25] In brief, Cameron made it clear that if Amery wanted to carry out the resolutions of the Governors' Conference he would have to send a direct order. Amery had reason to suspect that Cameron's position was supported by too many powerful men, particularly in the Labour Party, for such an action to be politic.

Sir Edward Grigg's most revealing statement about the conference, expressing his concern for the future and his awe of Cameron, is contained in a letter written in June. This communication was marked "Personal and Private" and addressed to "My Dear Leo." Such informality tells a great deal about

the relationship that existed between Grigg and Amery, as
compared with Cameron's official link with the Colonial
Secretary. Cameron did not feel free to write personal
letters about public policy to Amery and probably would
not have done so even if he and Amery had been good friends.
Part of Grigg's letter is worth quoting at some length
because it betrays Grigg's wonder at Cameron's surprising
attitude.

> He, Cameron, apparently draws a very hard and
> fast line between personal relations and official
> relations, and it is perfectly clear that on the
> official side he wants complete freedom from consul-
> tation or conference, so far as they can be secured.
> I think, in point of fact, that he regards Tanganyika
> as in some ways a peculiar and exceptional territory,
> responsible to other authorities outside the Empire
> as well as to the Imperial system with yourself as
> the controlling head. In talking with him I came
> again and again upon a sort of Chinese wall which
> he seems to draw round the Mandated Territory and
> which he appears to think essential to the adminis-
> trative progress on which his whole heart is set at
> the present time.[26]

Grigg's analysis was, of course, correct. Cameron understood
only too well the reality of Tanganyika's special position.
He stated later in defense of his policy that if Britain
could not honor the specifics of the mandate then "we should
say so openly, instead of silently ignoring our oblications
in this respect."[27] Unfortunately, Grigg could not understand that Tanganyika was a special case:

> I also cannot help resenting from the bottom of
> my soul any suggestion that the League of Nations has
> any superior authority to the British Empire, and
> higher standards to assert, or any right to interfere
> in what we may regard as the best system of organiza-
> tion and the best lines of policy for British East
> Africa as a whole.[28]

This is surely one of the most naive, emotionally based statements recorded by a colonial governor in the twentieth century.
The League did have "superior authority," and Cameron made this
fact the cornerstone of his approach to the Colonial Office.
    Another comment by Grigg on Cameron's attitude is even
more fantastic and shows even more clearly why Cameron found
it very difficult to work with the Kenya governor. He noted

that Cameron was an individualist, and continued,

> He has, of course, worked in that manner all his
> life, as Clifford's right hand man and I do not think
> that he understands the kind of team work which is
> absolutely essential if the Conference is to play any
> useful point in East African development.[29]

To imagine that Cameron did not understand fully what results
his actions might have was to completely misunderstand the
man. He was perfectly aware of what kind of power game he
was playing. Thus whether he was a "loner" or not was im-
material. He was not going to be a part of Grigg's team and
help secure the triumph of policies with which he disagreed.

One must look briefly at another of Grigg's charges before proceeding with further details of the debate over
closer union. Grigg maintained that much of Cameron's negative behavior was due to his mode of living. The Kenya
governor argued in the late 1920s and stressed again in his
book published almost thirty years later that Cameron was a
lonely man.[30] His implication was that, without friends or
confidants among his own staff, Cameron automatically adopted
a negative attitude toward Grigg's proposals. That the
Colonial Office at that time believed Cameron was motivated
largely by loneliness and spite is shown by Ormsby-Gore's
minute written in May 1926 where he noted,

> I gather from Dr. Oldham that Sir Donald is not
> in good health and is feeling the strain. He is
> really up against this office, openly expressed the
> opinion that the East African Commission's report is
> a mere hotch potch of Italian gossip, is very jealous
> of and antagonistic to Sir E. Grigg, and is evidently
> in a sorry state.[31]

This attitude toward Cameron shows how misinformed the
Colonial Office was as to his motivations. Cameron could dislike people with white-hot intensity and it is obvious that
he considered Grigg to be a pompous, inexperienced lackey,
but there is too much evidence available which shows that
Cameron's position vis à vis Grigg was taken on a matter of
principle. As already noted, Cameron was in all probability
a lonely man, but he had in his years in the Colonial Service
come to accommodate himself to this reality. To assert that
he acted against Grigg and Amery out of misanthropic loneliness is to ignore the corpus of his well-reasoned, logical
arguments against their pro-settler position. Furthermore,
any strain Cameron may have felt in 1926 came because, in
the midst of the complete reorganization of Tanganyika's

local government, he was forced to devote a large amount of time countering Amery's and Grigg's arguments for closer union.

Cameron's opposition, although castigated by Charles Strachey of the Colonial Office as "tiresome," helped postpone any immediate action toward closer union. Amery was also having problems in the ministry with Churchill and others who sought to embarrass him because of differences of opinion over the general strike. Without overwhelming support for closer union from East Africa, Amery did not dare chance a test of strength in the government, and he became convinced that the only way to secure his ends in East Africa was to persuade Cameron to abandon his opposition. This could be done either by argument or by having the affair thoroughly investigated by another commission whose report would presumably agree with the Colonial Secretary. In either case, nothing more could be done immediately. Even Lord Delamere was convinced that it would be fruitless to push for closer union in 1926. He thought that Cameron would have to be removed from office before the project was revived.[32]

One of the proposals that arose out of the issue of closer union was also deferred in 1926. This concerned the boundaries that divided the Masai. Lord Lugard had stated to the Mandates Commission that he favored bringing all the Masai together under one government. At the 1926 Governors' Conference, Grigg had noted the difficulties caused by the Masai and the need to have one set of operative rules concerning health, movement, and the carrying of weapons. To such proposals Cameron wrote what Ormsby-Gore termed a "redoubtable despatch" refuting most of the arguments for union. He showed that most of the Tanganyika Masai had no genuine viable political connections with their northern neighbors. They were aware that the Masai in Kenya were more closely controlled and paid a higher tax. Contrary to what Grigg had claimed, the government of Tanganyika had experienced few problems with the Masai, but Cameron believed that the Tanganyika Masai would resist any attempt to redraw the boundary in such a way as to place them under the jurisdiction of Kenya.[33] It is impossible to say whether Cameron's arguments or fears of a negative response from the League of Nations dissuaded Amery from pursuing the boundary question further. As the unexpected opposition to closer union developed, the Colonial Office became hesitant to venture too far without approval for the entire project. Eventually the proposal for boundary realignment between Kenya and Tanganyika was dropped.

Toward the end of 1926, Lord Lugard developed a scheme which he believed would satisfy the needs of all the contending factions in East Africa. He wanted to partition Kenya in such a way that the highlands would become primarily an area of white settlement. This area would then receive responsible government, whereas the African territories would continue to be ruled by the semi-autocratic style of Crown Colony government.[34] Although Lugard continued to pursue his plan with vigor over the next few years, few knowledgeable people took the plan seriously. This was because it obviously did not solve the problem of control of the coast, railroads, or labor supply, and offered no solution to the demands of the Indian community. But while the plan itself could be dismissed, its originator could not. Lugard wanted a settlement of the white highlands question as much as did Amery, Grigg, or Cameron. Thus the calm of late 1926 was not likely to last; some solution to the question of closer union had to come.

In September 1926, one issue was at last clarified. In most of the discussions and conferences on closer union, it was assumed that one or more of the British Central African possessions might become a part of the eventual federal union. In September the second unofficial conference of white settlers met. The delegates from Northern Rhodesia and Nyasaland made it clear that while they shared many problems common to the East African areas, they did not wish to be a part of any future political union with Kenya, Uganda, and Tanganyika.[35] After 1926, therefore, all serious discussions concerning closer union focused upon the three East African territories.

By early 1927, Sir Edward Grigg had abandoned the notion that closer union could be achieved in the form of immediate political association, with Kenya acting as the model for the new federal state. He evolved a new compromise plan which called for a federal council to control and coordinate transport, customs, communication, defense, and research. He did not favor any part of Lugard's plan for subdividing Kenya since he, too, believed this impractical. In order to obtain the approval of the white settler leaders for his plan, Grigg proposed that there should be an unofficial, although not wholly elected, majority in the proposed federal council. Amery in general approved of this new scheme and this was one of the reasons why he ordered Cameron to attend the Colonial Conference in mid-1927. Accompanied by Lady Cameron, Sir Donald left Tanganyika for Britain in April 1927. They traveled to Laurenco Marques and then to Johannesburg where they were kindly received by Prime Minister Hertzog. Just before leaving the Union, Cameron received orders from the Colonial Office to prepare a detailed statement of his views on closer union. Soon after his arrival in London he was informed that after the close of the Colonial Conference there would be a special series of meetings between the three governors and the Colonial Secretary on the subject of closer union.

Although the closer union controversy was the obvious
reason for Cameron's presence at the Colonial Conference, his
major contribution to the proceedings had nothing to do with
power politics, but rather in making suggestions which led
to the improvement of retirement benefits in the Colonial
Service. At the opening session of the conference, Cameron
brought out the need for standardization of the Colonial
Office pension plan. As with so much in the British government, the plan had grown to meet specific problems and contained many strange anomalies. If a man served all his time
in one territory at a median salary level, he might receive
a larger pension than someone who had been transferred and
promoted. The Colonial Office had promised to redesign the
plan as early as 1922, but had done little to carry out any
reform. Cameron was appointed chairman of a committee to
investigate and make recommendations to the Colonial Office.
Largely because of the report of this committee, the Colonial
Office adopted a system of reciprocity between territories,
the lack of which had been the great stumbling block to a
rational pension plan based on mixed service.[36]

The East Africa Governors' Conference took place in the
privacy of Amery's office after the larger Colonial Conference had adjourned. Once again it was Cameron who refused
to consider placing Tanganyika in an inferior position to
Kenya. He was fully aware of the support which he had from
the League of Nations, the Labour Party, and some of the
British colonial experts. On the other hand, many of the
theoreticians favored closer union. For example, Lord Lothain
and Lionel Curtis, ex-members of Lord Milner's kindergarten
and both propagandists for empire, supported Amery and Grigg.
But Cameron knew he could rely upon the backing of the bulk
of the Labour and Liberal members of the Commons and during
the course of the Governors' Conference he refused to budge
from his previous position. He also was particularly blunt
as to his opinion of the plan and of Governor Grigg. Presumably he overstepped what was considered decorous behavior
a number of times because he was rebuked sharply by the Permanent Undersecretary of the Colonial Office, Sir Samuel
Wilson, for making speeches directed at Grigg.[37] Cameron
simply would not compromise what he considered the well-
being of the Africans in his charge. He later wrote suc-
cintly of this period of political maneuvering that,

> The concept of the great white State was in
> jeopardy . . . not because of any native policy that
> may have been adopted in Tanganyika but because the
> gods there are have thought fit to place such a large
> and predominating proportion of Africans in these
> territories.[38]

At one juncture Cameron threatened to resign if Grigg's proposed plans were to be adopted over his objections. Lugard,
although generally favorably disposed toward Cameron's position, was shocked by such a threat. Obviously forgetting his
own propensity for high-handed action while Governor-General
of Nigeria, Lugard wrote to his wife,

> How times have changed! If Cameron had taken such
> a line with the S. of S. in the old days he would have
> been turned out and no-one would have been any wiser as
> to the reason. Now they simply darent . . . . The ad-
> vent of the Labour Party has its uses.[39]

The London conference between the governors and the
Secretary of State accomplished very little as a result of
Cameron's attitude and Amery's reluctance to force the issue.
He could not afford the notoriety of Cameron's resignation.
Grigg's plan along with the larger question of closer union
was submitted to a sub-committee for consideration. Its
recommendations were published as a white paper in July.[40]
Showing clearly the influence of the Colonial Secretary, the
report agreed that there was a clear necessity for closer
union particularly for the economic advantages it offered.
It stated the need for further investigations and called for
a new commission to be appointed to ascertain how closer
union might best be achieved. This report was the genesis
of the commission established in July 1927, and later named
after its chairman, Sir Hilton Young (later Lord Kennet of
Deane).

The Colonial Secretary himself appointed the chairman
and soon after doing so departed on a tour of the Commonwealth,
leaving his subordinates to fill out the rest of the commission. The members of the commission were of mixed backgrounds
and attitudes. Sir Hilton Young was a member of Parliament
and had been Secretary to the Treasury. The second member
was Sir George Schuster, a bank director and businessman, who
had served as Financial Secretary to the Sudan government.
Sir Reginald Mant, who had served in the Indian government,
was included perhaps to placate Indian opinion. The final
member, Dr. J. H. Oldham, was the Secretary of the International Missionary Council and was a friend of many colonial
administrators including Lord Lugard, but had no direct
African experience. In fact, only Schuster had served any
time in Africa. The composition of the commission, however,
could not be criticized too severely since its members, in
theory, necessarily represented diverse interest groups. The
Colonial Office rejected Grigg's suggestion that another
member, Sir Patrick Duncan, who had been one of Lord Milner's
associates in South Africa, be appointed. Grigg argued

reasonably that Duncan with great African experience, which included the position he then held as deputy to Prime Minister Smuts in South Africa, was sorely needed by the commission. He did not need to stress that Duncan would be predisposed toward the white settlers. Ormsby-Gore appears to have been the official most responsible for negating Grigg's proposal on the grounds that Duncan's addition would make the commission unnecessarily large.[41]

On 13 August 1927, in preparation for the visit of the Hilton Young Commission, Lord Delamere convened in Nairobi the third unofficial East African Conference. All British areas directly concerned with possible political union sent delegates, and despite the decision of the previous year to opt out of closer union, Northern and Southern Rhodesia were also represented, presumably because other issues such as labor and land policy were to be discussed. Kenya was heavily represented with thirteen delegates, and Sir Edward Grigg, although not present, sent his good wishes from South Africa. The speeches and resolutions were in general repetitious of previous meetings. Specifically, Tanganyika was criticized for its more stringent land sales policy to Europeans. Furthermore, the delegates wanted state aid to British settlers in Tanganyika so that German majorities which had developed in certain areas after 1925 could be reduced. The conference welcomed the Hilton Young Commission and unanimously recorded its support of federation for Kenya, Tanganyika, and Uganda.[42]

The Hilton Young Commission arrived in East Africa in January 1928. It spent ten days in Uganda, three weeks in Kenya, and a fortnight in Tanganyika. The commission did not present its findings until a year after its visit, and its conclusions were a disappointment for almost everyone.[43] There was a significant difference of opinion concerning closer union between the chairman who issued a minority report and the rest of the commission. The majority saw that great advantages could be gained from a political union of the three territories and recommended that steps be taken to effect an eventual federal union. It suggested that a chief executive for the proposed federation be appointed who at first would not be checked by any advisory council except the governors of the three territories and who would possess almost autocratic powers in legislating native policy. The commission's attempt to reconcile the wide differences of opinion concerning political union meant that the majority report was not acceptable to any significant power group in East Africa. To Cameron it spelled the surrender of his control over the rebuilding of traditional Native Authorities for the Africans of Tanganyika. Indian leaders in Kenya and Tanganyika were disturbed because the commission had not

recommended their equal representation with whites on the
territorial councils. The Kabaka of Buganda and other African leaders in Uganda preferred to negotiate native policy
directly with Whitehall rather than with a future High Commissioner with undefined substantive powers located in
Nairobi. Finally, the Kenya whites opposed the plan since
its implementation would have meant surrendering much of
their political power to the High Commissioner and would
have effectively ended their hopes for responsible government.

Sir Edward Grigg and Lord Delamere both viewed the report as a potential disaster. It did not discuss Lord Lugard's
plan for responsible government in the highlands nor did it
refer to the promise of white supremacy inherent in Winston
Churchill's declaration of 1922.[44] However, the commissioners
had congratulated Cameron and the Tanganyika administration
on its native policy. The report had also recommended a
common electoral roll for Indians and Europeans in Kenya and
suggested that Africans as soon as possible be given political equality on the central legislatures. Much later Amery,
forgetting perhaps his role in creating the atmosphere in
which the commission worked, also criticized the members for
"not confining themselves to the economic issues."[45]

The negative reaction to the Hilton Young report from
so many quarters would have convinced most men to give up the
quest for political union. However, Amery was not so easily
dissuaded from his objective. Much to Cameron's disgust, he
was called to London toward the end of 1928 to discuss with
Grigg and Amery the implications of the Hilton Young report.
To a casual observer in 1926, it seemed that nothing could
stop the unification of East Africa and Cameron was a lonely
voice in British officialdom crying out against Amery's
schemes. But during the next two years Cameron's position
had been bolstered by the support of powerful sections of the
Labour and Liberal parties, and now even many Conservatives
were questioning Amery's forcing of the issue. At the conferences in January and February 1929, Cameron again refused
to retreat from his position that Britain had accepted the
Tanganyika mandate on conditions that would not admit of the
type of closer union being proposed. He again threatened to
resign and openly canvased members of Parliament for their
support.[46]

The only tangible result of the 1929 conference between
the Secretary of State, Cameron, and Grigg was the decision
to send the Permanent Undersecretary of State, Sir Samuel
Wilson, to East Africa. Wilson was to try to pinpoint the
areas where greater cooperation could be fostered and to
determine on what type of closer association (and on what

terms) would be acceptable to the diverse groups in the three
territories. Cameron conferred with Wilson while he was in
Dar es Salaam. Later there was a meeting in Nairobi between
Cameron, Gowers, Wilson, and the acting Governor of Kenya.
The positions of the protagonists were not changed by this
new round of conferences. Considering these attitudes and
the climate of opinion created by the Hilton Young report,
it is a tribute to Wilson that he was able to frame proposals
which Sir Philip Mitchell stated were not dissimilar to those
finally put into effect in 1948.[47] However, Wilson's proposals came at a bad time, and any action to implement them was
postponed until after the general election of 9 June 1929,
which the Conservatives felt sure of winning. However, the
Labour Party gained enough seats to enable it in cooperation
with the Liberals to form its second government in the twentieth century. The new government had a different view of
colonial responsibilities from that of the previous Conservative administration. It was not favorably disposed toward
any schemes which would be likely to confirm the political
supremacy of white minorities. In addition, Lord Passfield,
who became Secretary of State for the Colonies, was deeply
suspicious of the motives of white settlers in East Africa
and was personally opposed toward Amery's plans.

In June 1929, in the midst of the high-level debates
relating to the needs and desires of the white settlers and
Africans in Tanganyika, Cameron began a tour of the northern
areas for the first time since November 1926. This long absence of the governor from the areas of white settlement was
a minor contribution to the strained relations between him
and the Europeans in Tanganyika. Although untrue, the white
settlers believed that he had deliberately avoided meeting
them and listening to their complaints. During his two-month
tour in 1929, Cameron visited representatives of European
planter groups in all the major centers. Only at Moshi did
he find open, undisguised hostility. The encounter there on
22 July between the governor and the six representatives of
the local branch of the European association came to be called
the Moshi Incident.[48] Cameron had agreed to meet them to
discuss only one item--the possibility of participation of
non-officials in the local government in Tanga and the Northern Province. The president of the association, Mr. Pinaar,
who had been described as a kindly old Afrikaner, ostensibly
led the settler delegation, but the actual spokesman was Mr.
de la Mothe, the general secretary. De la Mothe was brutally
frank in expressing his opinions. He refused to admit that
Cameron had agreed to discuss only one item and claimed that
it was understood that the meeting was to discuss the full
range of their complaints concerning land, labor, and political representation as reflected in a petition they had
presented to Cameron two days before.

The governor was accompanied by Provincial Commissioner
Webster, District Officer Dawkins, and four other government
officers. They, however, remained silent during the conference unless asked for some specific information by the governor. The dialogue between Sir Donald and de la Mothe was
extremely bitter. Reading the transcript of the meeting over
forty years later, one can appreciate why Cameron's colleagues
and subordinates recoiled from his cutting remarks. He did
not attempt to be diplomatic with de la Mothe, but indicated
that he believed the white settlers to be dishonest in putting
together their petition. He stated that they attributed to
him anti-settler sentiments he did not hold. The fact that
he opposed their desire to dominate the land and force the
African onto the labor market did not mean that he was unaware
of the problems of Europeans or their potential contribution
to the territory. De la Mothe on his part accused Cameron
of playing the demigod surrounded by junior officers who were
afraid of him. He clearly implied that the governor did not
want consultation with anyone who might disagree with his
policies; instead he believed Cameron wanted to rule Tanganyika
as a large personal estate.

The meeting at Moshi settled nothing and is important
in retrospect only because the discussions between Cameron
and de la Mothe delineated very well, in undiplomatic language,
the differences between the governor and the white settlers.
Cameron in two and a half years of debate with endless cham-
pions of white supremacy had grown tired of their arguments.
As he had stated before, he was not adverse to white colonization of certain parts of Tanganyika if the settlers understood that the mandate government meant African paramountcy.
The bulk of Cameron's work had gone into constructing a viable
system of indirect rule and he would not be lectured to by
Amery or Grigg, and certainly not by a man such as de la Mothe
whom he considered a rank opportunist.

The European settlers mystified Cameron. He later wrote,

> I never got quite to the bottom of the business
> side of the settlers in the northern province. Except
> for the pioneers who settled in the German era, they
> have bought their land very cheap at the sale of ex-
> enemy properties, but, speaking generally, they did
> not seem to be making any great profit out of the cul-
> tivation of coffee, the staple crop, when I was in the
> territory. Some of them were making money; others not
> much more than a rather bare subsistence.[49]

He went on to speculate that one reason for their poor showing and hence their fear of African competition stemmed from

63

a fact of geography. Much of the land the Germans had confiscated from the Africans on the slopes of Mt. Kilamanjaro was at a median level. The land they had left for the Chagga at a higher elevation proved to be much more favorable for the growing of Arabica coffee than the lower-level European farms.

Returning to a consideration of the larger issue of closer union, one can ask how important Cameron was in changing the opinions of British officials during 1929. According to Philip Mitchell who was the Secretary for Native Affairs and one of the governor's closest confidants, Cameron said, after returning from England in April, that "he had fixed Amery, but had had to mobilize Ramsay MacDonald, Baldwin, J. H. Thomas, the late Archbishop and the Lord knows who." Cameron, in telling Mitchell this, "was in great form and plainly enjoyed his venture into privy conspiracy."[50]

In the following month, May 1929, Cameron proposed a scheme of devolution designed to placate the feelings of the white settlers in Tanganyika and further separate them from their fellows in Kenya. He suggested that an officer be appointed as the governor's representative who would live permanently at the governor's lodge at Arusha. This officer would move around the northern areas and his main function would be to insure better communications between the settlers and the governor in Dar es Salaam. Cameron also proposed the creation of consultative district committees which could help the governor in preparing legislation affecting the settlers. Amery did not act on Cameron's suggestions, and after the change of government in Britain Cameron resubmitted this proposal to Passfield who turned it down, giving as his reason that he did not wish to compromise the larger issue of closer union.[51]

The Labour government in fact decided to submit the entire question of closer union to further scrutiny by appointing a Joint Committee of both Houses of Parliament. The idea was so reasonable on the surface, but given the realities of the East African question, the Joint Committee would only postpone a definite decision. Who first thought of this new investigation? There is every reason to believe that the scheme was Cameron's brainchild. Mitchell wrote that Cameron while in London on leave "had started an entirely new hare," the Joint Committee.[52] With the appointment of the committee it was obvious to all that the tide had turned and that it was Cameron, not Grigg, who had the friends in high places. The committee was composed of members of Parliament who were committed by previous pronouncements not to act in ways they considered detrimental to the African. By this time, also, permanent officials in the Colonial Office had finally arrived at a conclusion that they should have reached three years before. As Sir Samuel Wilson succinctly put it, "Sir

D. Cameron doesn't really want any form of closer union
whether economic or otherwise." Wilson's comment was in a
minute replying to a statement in Sir Donald's dispatch of
16 August 1929. In this Cameron had written that coordina-
tion of common services such as posts and railroads was
"comparatively of no importance." What was important to
Cameron was that the government refrain from implementing
certain policies "before general principles have been
affirmed."53

Before the Joint Committee had completed its investigations, the Labour government issued a white paper in 1930
which ostensibly was to form a basis for further discussion.54
Little new was introduced in the white paper, and the re-
stressing of the need for a High Commissioner renewed the
fears of most of the various factions in East Africa. In
the spring and summer of 1931, after Cameron had left Tanganyika, delegations from each area and representatives of
each community gave evidence before the Joint Committee.
The weight of evidence presented to the Joint Committee was
against any form of closer union. In Tanganyika the white
settlers indicated that they were willing to accept Wilson's
proposals, but the majority of those in Kenya did not want
an autocratic High Commissioner. Africans from Tanganyika
joined their counterparts in the other territories, particularly those of Uganda, in opposing any shift of power
away from their own governor. In general the African representatives indicated their satisfaction with the attempts
of the administrators to develop the system of indirect
rule.

Considering all the trouble and expense the government
had gone to, the recommendations of the Joint Committee were
not exactly earthshaking. It decided that there was no
general agreement that would make a form of closer union
acceptable and workable. It advised that common post,
telegraph, and customs systems and excise taxes be continued, as should the Governors' Conference. The onset of
the world-wide depression was obviously a factor in the
government's decision not to force an unpopular concept
upon the people of East Africa. However, in retrospect,
closer union appears to have been a dead issue when the
Labour Party was returned to power in 1929. Lord Passfield
was unlikely to override the considered arguments of Sir
Donald Cameron, a man whom the Secretary of State admired
and trusted.

In assessing this important phase of Cameron's career,
one cannot escape the important non-historical question of
whether his policy was correct. Sir Philip Mitchell was
later critical of Cameron's inflexible attitude and believed
that some form of closer union should have been tried. The
disagreement between Cameron and Mitchell over this issue

became so bitter that the governor had no contact with his Secretary for Native Affairs, aside from strictly official matters, for the last three months of their association.[55] Mitchell also considered that Amery was primarily responsible for the failure of the scheme because he did not use the power and prestige of his office to force some type of closer union.[56] Despite Mitchell's opinion and the obvious fact that unification would have solved many British administrative and economic problems in the two decades after Cameron's departure, it is doubtful whether the League of Nations would have allowed an imposition of a federal structure of the type envisioned by Grigg and Delamere in 1926. In any case, after 1927 Amery was in no position to act the role of the autocrat. As to the potential viability of closer union, the history of an independent Nigeria in the 1960s shows that an arbitrary and unnatural creation of a large unitary or federal state does not necessarily aid Africans in solving their most pressing problems. More important, in the context of the 1920s, it is difficult to see how Cameron could have accepted any of the plans for closer union without accepting their corollary of white supremacy. Cameron saw clearly that his plans for educating Africans for eventual self-government depended upon keeping them free from the subservient position they occupied in Kenya. His victory over the adherents of closer union was a guarantee that his system of indirect rule would be given time to mature. The defeat of Amery and Grigg thus protected the embryo Native Authority system, Cameron's greatest contribution to Tanganyika.

5

Revision of Tanganyika Local Government

Sir Donald Cameron's most lasting contribution to Africa was his redefinition of indirect rule and its application first to Tanganyika and later in reorganizing the government of Nigeria. Despite his great contribution to the theory and practice of African local government, it should be remembered that forms of indirect rule were in general practice throughout British Africa by the mid-1920s. In Tanganyika, Governor Byatt's Native Authority Ordinances had created a type of hybrid system where traditional elements were allowed some scope within what was still basically the Akida system. Cameron later stated that he did not come to Tanganyika "itching to introduce the Nigerian system of Indirect Rule" since while in Nigeria he had not belonged to the group "which blindly worshipped" the system.[1] However, given the conditions in Tanganyika, the popularity of schemes of indirect rule with the Colonial Office, and Cameron's own background, it would have been surprising if Sir Donald had tried to introduce any other system.

The first major reform of Byatt's system of local government made by Cameron was the revision of the taxing system. The largest single source of revenue for the Tanganyika government was the combined hut and poll tax which in the 1920s averaged a levy of approximately ten shillings annually per adult male. In addition, adult taxpayers could be called upon to provide services and in some cases tribute to their local rulers.[2] Governor Byatt had been aware of the inequity of this system which amounted to dual taxation of the African. In March 1924, he had suggested that the government commute the chiefs' privileges.[3] Cameron's role in altering the taxing system was merely to follow up Byatt's suggestion and to fill out the skeleton of the proposal with concrete provisions. Cameron later noted a further reason why it was imperative to abolish the chiefs' prerogatives. Despite the services rendered to them, the authority of the native rulers was undermined by having the hut and poll tax collected by district officers. He remarked further that the people of the territory seldom saw British officials unless they were collecting taxes.[4]

With Colonial Office approval, Cameron in late 1925 abolished the system of tribute and services, substituting in their place a fixed amount of remuneration for the rulers.

This solution, however, carried with it the danger of making the African rulers only a certain type of official directly dependent for their salary on the central authorities, which would have undermined their authority even further. Attempting to avoid such a possibility, Cameron established a fund from the collected taxes for a kind of civil list in each native area. Stipends were determined by the relative importance of the rulers and were paid from the fund. Any amount left over after the salaries were paid could then be applied to improving the conditions of the people in a given area. Thus Sir Donald laid the foundation for a system of Native Treasuries.[5] Cameron's plan was that once the Native Authority system became better organized, the rulers or their deputies would be made responsible for collecting the hut and poll tax. Rebates could then be made to these local treasuries of the Native Authorities. Africans themselves could thus be directly involved in the area of government most important to them and they could plan for and carry out their own development schemes. Cameron hoped that the rebates could be increased to the point where they would equal half the total tax collected. The following chart indicates how far this concept had been realized before the onset of the depression ruined all chances of such devolution.[6]

Year	Tax collected (£)	Rebates (£)
1925-26	674,973	99,337
1926-27	682,106	120,304
1927-28	708,533	133,014
1928-29	736,970	145,956
1929-30	748,734	152,818
1930-31	700,852	157,124

The major constraint on the system of taxation and Native Treasuries evolved by Cameron was the scarcity of funds for all services in Tanganyika. Despite his commitment to establishing workable Native Treasuries where Africans could learn to manage their own finances, he was never able to give them more than 20 percent of the tax collected. Most of this sum went to pay the salaries of the officials involved in the administration of the Native Authorities. The combined budget of all the Native Treasuries for Tanganyika Territory for the year 1929-30 shows how little money was left for vital services after salaries had been paid. Tribal administration received £122,098, but medical services only £16,830, education £13,317, agriculture £7,768, and roads and bridges £9,425.[7]

It soon became apparent to Cameron that the old subdivisions of Tanganyika drawn by the Germans were inadequate. The senior administrative officers in their Dar es Salaam meeting had already noted that the entire local government structure needed to be completely overhauled. To do this intelligently the central authorities would have to investigate traditional authorities in all parts of Tanganyika. However, within three weeks of his arrival Cameron decided to deal with the question of the chiefs' stipends in lieu of salary--a problem whose solution was long overdue--and this forced him to consider the forms of local government much earlier than he had intended. He very quickly decided to continue some type of indirect rule throughout Tanganyika. Administrative expediency was obviously the major reason for this decision, but apart from this he had two other reasons for his actions. He later wrote,

> I believed that the people would in addition derive material as well as moral advantage from it. ... I hoped to afford a means acceptable to the African that would build up his sense of responsibility and in the long run make him proud of being a member of his own society.[8]

But few European officers had any detailed knowledge of the African societies they administered. To remedy this defect Cameron soon after arriving in Tanganyika ordered the district officers to make detailed surveys of their areas to determine quickly what the Native Authorities of Tanganyika actually were. The district authorities were instructed to ascertain whether indigenous tribal institutions had survived during European occupation and rule, and to report their findings as soon as possible to Dar es Salaam.

Cameron's major preoccupation throughout the year after his arrival was surveying the growing body of data on Native Authorities and seeing that wherever possible traditional leaders were recognized by the government. He was also deeply involved in revising Lugard's Political Memoranda for issue to all district officers. Cameron's main collaborator in writing these "little brown books" was Philip Mitchell who was also the man most responsible for getting the Native Authority system into operation. When the books were issued they became "the Bible" of administrative practice for junior officers. In fact these detailed books on Native Authority procedure were so successful in Tanganyika that they were later revised and reprinted for use in Nigeria, and Sir H. Richmond Palmer reissued them as guides for district officers in the Gambia. One of the points Cameron continually stressed was how mischievous it was for a European to assume too much on the basis of superficial evidence:

> It is ensnaring and dangerous to proceed on the assumption that this or that must have been the tradition and custom of a people; that they must at some time have obeyed this or that authority of their own. The present generation is possibly quite ignorant of such tradition; it is they that are primarily concerned and we must be quite certain before constituting an authority on such a basis that they are going to recognize and obey its orders.[9]

Despite Cameron's understanding of the complexities of a traditional system among any one group of people, he was forced into doing what he warned against. He had to arrive at definite conclusions about the traditional systems as quickly as possible. In Bukoba, Sukumaland, Uchagga, Iringa, and Usambara organized minor states were still functioning, but in many places there were only disrupted clan and village authorities. Along the coast the only viable type of government appeared to be the Akida system introduced by the Arabs and continued by the Europeans. In spite of the problems, Cameron pressed on with gazetting Native Authorities. He kept a large map of Tanganyika on which each new Native Authority was indicated in red. By the end of Cameron's second year all but two districts had been colored.[10]

Certain ad hoc methods of recognizing a traditional ruler were followed by the government authorities. Cameron needed as a first step local governments that the people would obey. He said that at the beginning "so far as we could and need go into the matter for the time being we knew this, namely, that if a people continue to render tribute and service to a particular man it was fairly safe to assume for the time being that they recognized him as their chief in accordance with native custom."[11] It is not surprising that many errors were made in establishing indirect rule when district officers, fully aware of the necessity for speed in finding and setting up the new Native Authorities, were forced to act as amateur anthropologists. Cameron's insistence upon establishing Native Authorities no matter how weak they might be brought the greatest amount of criticism from veteran district officers. They knew that in districts where there were no strong traditional rulers the men chosen to be chiefs would be so in name only. The district officer would have to continue to rule directly, but with the added burden of trying to make it appear that the African rulers were making the decisions.[12] In most of the places where mistakes were made

Cameron could be exonerated since he did not regard the system in any locale as final. The conclusions reached for any given people, he believed, should be continually reexamined.

While the field staff was spending most of its time in 1925 gathering information, Cameron had partially reorganized the central administration. His major reform was the creation of the post of Secretary for Native Affairs to act as the governor's chief advisor and spokesman on African affairs. The secretary was a member of both the Legislative and Executive Councils and had complete access to all papers at Government House related to local government. However, he functioned free of the administrative hierarchy because his office did not act as a stop in communication between the provincial commissioners and the governor. An additional advantage to this type of structuring was that the Secretary for Native Affairs was freed from much routine paperwork so that he could spend the bulk of his time traveling throughout the territory and overseeing the establishment and functioning of the new Native Authority system.[13] Cameron was fortunate in the men who first occupied this sensitive post. Charles Dundas served as Secretary for Native Affairs until 1928 when he was succeeded in this post by his deputy, Philip Mitchell. Both men had long experience in supervising African governments, both were extremely capable, with practical views which could translate theory into reality, and both believed in Cameron and his plans for the future of Tanganyika.

Sir Donald maintained that before instituting any of the changes in native administration he consulted the senior officers who would be directly concerned with the altered system. From Cameron's vantage point this was undoubtedly true. He traveled much more than had his predecessor and he did consult Dundas, Mitchell, and his provincial officers. However, in asserting later the consensus he found among his subordinates he had forgotten the rituals of the pecking order in the Colonial Service. Few men in subordinate positions would readily disagree openly with any governor. Cameron's austere personality, his reputation, and caustic tongue also acted to dissuade all but a few from opposing his ideas. There were only a few provincial officers and senior district officers who disagreed with Cameron and a number of these disliked him intensely. According to the testimony of many persons who served under Cameron, they only grumbled that the new governor did not know what he was doing. The very young men in the service tended to view Cameron with reverence and awe as a distant figure whose orders were to be obeyed. Until some of them came to work at the Secretariat in Dar es Salaam, most were in no position to alter this opinion and they simply carried out orders

71

to institute indirect rule in their districts. The senior
officers who caused them the most fear were Dundas and Mitchell whom they could expect to meet often and who could look
around their districts asking very embarrassing questions.[14]

The major piece of legislation by which Cameron accomplished the changes in Tanganyika's local government was the
Native Authority Ordinance of 1926, although many changes had
already been instituted under the authority of the Ordinance
of 1923.[15] A close comparison of the two ordinances shows
that Cameron altered very little of the earlier enabling
legislation; most of the changes he made were procedural.
The major alteration was that the Ordinance of 1926 provided
for a hierarchy of Native Authorities, with both superior and
subordinate authorities being recognized. The difference
then between Byatt's and Cameron's approach toward local
government lies not in the realm of legislation. It was in
the different attitude of Cameron's administration toward
the necessity of recognizing viable African governmental institutions. Cameron wanted reforms, and his lieutenants in
the field, reflecting this urgency, pushed forward with them.

In searching for models for establishment of indirect
rule both Lugard and Cameron had looked toward India. The
one major difference between the views of the two men was
that Lugard tended to view the Indian system in terms of the
actions and responsibilities of the princes, while Cameron
thought the key to the system was the panchayat or village
council. This difference was fundamental. Lugard and most
of his successors in Nigeria were uncomfortable when confronting African systems where there were no chiefs. Cameron on
the other hand was concerned with determining the traditional
mechanisms of rule. He was prepared to accept and recognize
the validity of very small Native Authorities. He hoped
that in time, with the proper guidance, they could evolve
toward viable larger groupings. In Tanganyika, Cameron
recognized four differing types of Native Authority all of
which were supposed to derive their authority from the
people and their traditions. These were (a) federation of
chiefs, (b) chiefs, (c) tribal councils, and (d) independent headmen.[16]

The Native Authority Ordinance of 1926 conferred very
definite powers on the Native Authorities. They had full
power of arrest for crimes committed within their jurisdiction. They could issue orders, which were binding, concerning such specific items as the manufacturing and sale of
liquor, possession of weapons, gambling, and theft. The
ordinance also gave the authorities jurisdiction over projects that might require the use of a considerable amount
of manpower such as certain land conservation projects or

fighting natural disasters like the incursion of locusts.
The power of the district officers was in theory restricted
because they were specifically prohibited from issuing orders
on matters under Native Authority jurisdiction unless the
authority had failed to act in a crucial situation. Until
the close of World War II this remained only theoretical in
many parts of Tanganyika where the chiefs continued to depend
upon the district officers' decisions.[17]

Correlate with the expansion of the low-level executive
and legislative powers given by Cameron's administration to
traditional authorities was the attempt to increase their
judicial powers. The existing legislation passed during
Byatt's tenure was adequate for the establishment of Native
Courts. However, apart from Mohammedan courts in some urban
areas, few courts had actually been established by the end of
1924. With many Tanganyika groups, as was the case with so
many African tribes, executive and judicial authority were
considered to be one. What the Germans and the British had
done either by design or inadvertence was to separate officially the two complementary functions. Obviously wherever
traditional authority had survived, even in a greatly modified form, the leaders had continued to exercise some of
their judicial prerogatives without official sanction.

During the first year of Cameron's administration there
was a very rapid expansion of the Native Courts system.
Elders or chiefs of recognized Native Authorities were
encouraged to practice customary law wherever possible.
Native Authorities on their own or acting through or with
the district officer were empowered to make rules and regulations over certain functions. Once this had been done the
Native Authority was given jurisdiction in enforcing the new
edicts. Traditional rulers were also made responsible for
judging certain types of offenders who had broken laws generally applicable to the entire territory. Cameron believed
that by recognizing the juridical rights of a Native Authority he could not only restore old equilibriums but also
force African law into adapting to changing conditions.
A further alteration in the rules of the Native Courts bolstered the Native Treasuries. Until 1925 fees and fines in
the Native Courts went to a fund administered by the district
officer. This practice was changed to divert these increasing sums for use by the Native Authority.[18]

Throughout 1926 while in the midst of the struggle over
closer union, Cameron and his staff systematically constructed
a new administrative system which would provide for the greatest flexibility in loosely controlling the Native Authorities.
On 1 January 1927, the existing twenty-two districts established by the Germans gave way to a new structure of eleven

73

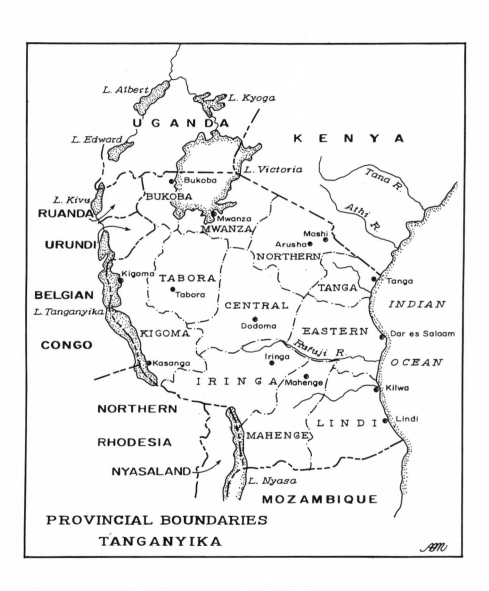

L. Albert

L. Kyoga

UGANDA

KENYA

L. Edward

L. Victoria

Tana R.

Bukoba

BUKOBA

Athi R.

L. Kivu

RUANDA

Mwanza

MWANZA

Moshi

Arusha

URUNDI

NORTHERN

Kigoma

TABORA

TANGA

Tanga

BELGIAN

Tabora

CENTRAL

INDIAN

L. Tanganyika

Dodoma

EASTERN

Dar es Salaam

CONGO

KIGOMA

Iringa

Rufuji R.

OCEAN

Kasanga

IRINGA

Mahenge

Kilwa

NORTHERN

LINDI

Lindi

RHODESIA

MAHENGE

NYASALAND

L. Nyasa

MOZAMBIQUE

PROVINCIAL BOUNDARIES

TANGANYIKA

provinces each under the direction of a provincial officer.
These eleven provinces were further subdivided into forty-
two districts each in the charge of a district officer.[19]
Much of the power previously centered in Dar es Salaam was
devolved on the provincial officers. They were given great
discretionary powers over native affairs even in time re-
placing the Tanganyika High Court as the supervisory power
over Native Courts. The chart below shows in more detail the
organization of the Tanganyika government in 1929.[20]

Organization of Government of Tanganyika, 1929

Provinces	Districts	Area in square miles	Estimated population	Headquarters
Mwanza	Mwanza, Maswa, Musoma, Kwimba	25,530	789,647	Mwanza
Bukoba	Bukoba, Biharamulo	11,010	348,036	Bukoba
Tabora	Tabora, Kahama, Nzega, Shinyanga	40,230	533,746	Tabora
Kigoma	Kigoma, Kasulu, Kibondo, Ufpia	48,345	290,519	Kigoma
Iringa	Iringa, Njombe, Rungwe, Mbeya	41,450	413,882	Iringa
Mahenge	Mahenge, Songea	32,730	197,572	Mahenge
Lindi	Lindi, Mikindani, Kilwa, Masasi	38,910	357,255	Lindi
Eastern	Dar es Salaam, Rufiji, Bagamoyo, Morogoro, Kilosa	27,320	519,216	Dar es Salaam
Central	Dodoma, Singida, Kondoa, Manyoni	38,770	607,467	Dodoma
Tanga	Tanga, Usambara, Pangani, Handeni, Pare	13,863	349,375	Tanga
Northern	Arusha, Masai, Mbulu, Moshi	33,770	324,991	Arusha

The institution of the new administrative system in
combination with Cameron's views toward local government
wrought revolutionary changes in Tanganyika. There were,
admittedly, a great number of mistakes made by the government

and it is obvious that the new system was not, in all places,
a reflection of traditional rule. But Cameron with his
Nigerian background and Mitchell from his experience and
travel in South Africa were convinced of the justice of their
reforms and went to apply their theories as Mitchell said,
"with the enthusiasm of religious revivalists."[21] The very
speed of the application of the Native Authority system
meant errors. At first there were great jealousies between
headmen in certain areas, and many of these had not been
completely surveyed. Cameron, Dundas, and Mitchell began
almost immediately after the institution of a Native Authority to review and reevaluate the districts and their leaders.
By this process, considerable change had been effected in
the size and number of Native Authorities throughout Tanganyika by 1929. Some of these changes had been made to correct
earlier errors of assessment, but more were the result of
government pressure to create larger, more viable administrations. Cameron seems to have underestimated his power to
influence decisions by African leaders. Mitchell noted that
the Sukuma chiefs, when they found out that the governor
wanted them to agree to any policy, would do so without having any ideas of the consequences of their actions.[22] Nevertheless, by 1929 many of the errors of the earlier district-
ing had been corrected, and thanks to the knowledge of Dundas
and Mitchell, most of the amalgamated authorities had been
kept within the boundaries of traditional political life.
The following chart shows how far consolidation had gone by
the end of 1929.[23]

Province	No. of units after first introduction of Indirect Admin- istration	No. as of 31 Dec. 1929	Remarks
Bukoba	6	6	
Central	15	8	
Eastern	18	18	Does not include Dar es Salaam
Iringa	15	13	
Kigoma	16	13	
Lindi	21	17	
Mahenge	11	9	
Mwanza	32	23	
Northern	10	9	
Tabora	33	13	
Tanga	15	5	Does not include Tanga District
	192	134	

Cameron's system obviously worked better in those sections of Tanganyika where the traditional structures had not been severely damaged. In some areas, notably Bukoba District with nine superior and fifty-one subordinate authorities and in much of the Mwanza Province, the new structures were almost immediately accepted by the people as a natural extension of their traditional system. However, even among the Bukoba the Native Authorities were not merely a reconstruction of the indigenous method of rule. The chiefs (Bakama) of Bukoba, all of them Hima nobles, in 1925 would only sit together in the same room on the condition that they be allowed to sit with their back to one another.[24] Cameron, despite his willingness to accept many small authorities, was convinced that the Bukoba had much in common and should be pushed by the central government to recognize that fact.

The first Provincial Commissioner to Bukoba under Cameron was F. W. Brett who had been an active participant in the 1924 Dar es Salaam Conference. Once appointed, he immediately began to apply his principles of indirect rule to Bukoba. Earlier the government had promised the Bakama that their revenues would remain at the level established by the Germans. Brett believed that the income of the Bakama actually was too high since it was sometimes illicitly derived from wealth created by government investment. The Bakama do not appear to have raised any great objections to their share of the new tax rate and even the reduction of their tribute to a token one shilling compensation. What did disturb the chiefs was the belated realization that payments would be made on a monthly basis from a central treasury. Brett wanted to curb the position of the Bakama since he did not believe that the Bakoba rulers upheld their weight in the administration of the country and therefore he established a central Native Treasury at the end of 1925. The African placed in charge of the treasury had formerly been a clerk under both the German and British administrations. His function was that of the administrative sub-accountant who had previously dispensed tax rebates to the Bakama. The central treasury clearly placed the Bakama under bureaucratic control. The chiefs' income came from a variety of monthly payments, fixed payments, the lukikos (Bakama courts), and the gombololas (sub-chief courts). The courts paid their fees and fines into the central Native Treasury and in return they received a fixed monthly amount which was used to pay the salaries of the clerk and messenger policemen. The Bakama remained responsible for the collection of taxes and the enforcement of a variety of social and economic measures, although the European administration took over the registration of taxpayers.

All Brett's reforms are indications of an attempt to
get the Bakama to assume more responsibility toward government, but even more they represent the extension of a greater
amount of control by the central bureaucracy over traditional
native life. To carry out all their new responsibilities
the chiefs had to maintain fairly large staffs of clerks and
messengers, and in 1926 there was introduced a Bakama Council
(Kiama) which was to meet monthly under the supervision of
the district officers for deliberation of general policy.
In the context of traditional Haya politics, such an institution was revolutionary since encounters between active rulers
of different kingdoms were supposed to be fatally dangerous.
However, previous European rule had undermined this belief
and had shown the Bakama that they indeed had a number of
things in common with one another. One of the problems that
arose was that no single chief would in any way allow another
to be designated paramount over him, and so there was an
accepted lack of leadership in the council which tended to
inhibit its effectiveness. As one historian of the Bukoba
has noted, "Indeed, in many cases council meetings were used
by the administration as a platform on which to lecture the
Bakama on measures alien to their understanding and the
chiefs themselves seemed to have taken a spontaneous interest
only in questions immediately relevant to their personal
interest."[25]

In many areas of Tanganyika, such as Bukoba, the facade
of the indigenous system was maintained while the central
government altered it almost beyond recognition. In other
areas the reorganization gave the traditional rulers much
more political power than they had ever enjoyed before.
This was particularly noticeable among the Masai where their
Laibon was granted full authority as a paramount chief even
though he had previously never possessed much temporal authority.[26]

Robert Heussler, who has produced the most detailed
analysis of the role of district officers in Tanganyika, dis-
cusses a number of areas where the new system operated reasonably well. Despite differences in their composition, the
Native Authorities in Iringa Province performed better than
expected by the provincial commissioner. Kwimba District of
Mwanza Province was an area where there was good cooperation
between the district officers, chiefs, and headmen. In general Heussler is very critical of the functioning of Cameron's
system, particularly in territories where the political structure was weak or where those institutions had been disrupted
by war or repression. In such places the district officers,
always mindful of the pecking order, wrote reports which would

assure the provincial commissioner and the central authorities that all was working according to plan. The reality often was direct rule by the district officer, only faintly disguised by his reports when it was necessary to justify a system he did not believe in.[27]

It was in the coastal districts that Cameron's ideas met their greatest test and where the failure of his system was most noticeable. Here the Arabs had influenced African rule for centuries and had governed directly in many places for over one hundred years. The Germans and later the British had not made any direct moves to alter the political structures devised by the Sultan of Zanzibar. The method of rule there was the Akida system which to Cameron represented the worst evils of the old non-traditional political authorities. Cameron refused to admit that along the coast, with all the mixing of population and cultures combined with generations of foreign control, there could be no discernable types of traditional rule. The fact was that in some places such as the Bagamoyo area the incumbent Akidas had held their positions since before the "scramble." Nevertheless, Cameron ordered Dundas and his subordinate officers to search out these sleeping political structures and refused to allow the coastal districts to retain their Akidas, though he was finally persuaded by his European staff to allow the important towns to keep the Liwales. Thus Cameron in preparing the way for his reforms of coastal government abandoned his pragmatic attitude and assumed a dogmatism that was unusual of the man.

In retrospect Cameron's chief lieutenant and perhaps foremost disciple, Philip Mitchell, admitted that "we made many mistakes and got many things wrong," and he considered that the greatest of the errors was Cameron's attitude toward the Akidas of the coast. By Sir Donald's adamant stand the government lost the services of a considerable number of experienced men, and by dismissing them dealt unjustly with these otherwise faithful servants. A second detrimental effect of Cameron's position was that it became necessary for the provincial and district officers to uncover "traditional" authorities. In many cases the Europeans simply "found" indigenous leaders to fill the newly created councils.[28]

Why did Cameron violate his own rules in dealing with the Coast? There can be no definitive answer to this question, but it is clear that he believed he had acted only after due consultation with his chief subordinates. He had listened to their opinions and then made the decision he thought best. One must give great weight to the pertinent comment made by Mitchell who noted that Cameron did not really know very much about Africans and the details of their everyday lives.[29]

This seems a shocking statement to make in discussing the
contributions of one of the great governors of British Africa,
but it is possible to be blinded to the most obvious facts
by the reputation of an administrator such as Lugard or
Cameron. In all probability Cameron did not know the subtle
differences that distinguished one group of tribal Africans
from another. Mitchell or Dundas, because they had served
as district officers working in close association with
Africans, knew much more about the people of Tanganyika than
did the governor. Because of his intelligence and quick
grasp of a problem, Sir Donald always gave the impression of
knowing much more about African societies than he actually
did. He had spent only a brief period in the field and that
had been in Nigeria fifteen years before. Cameron had a
deep-seated conviction that African traditional rule, in
whatever form, suited Africans better than any foreign system
imposed on them. He was equally opposed to either autocratic
or democratic principles that did not spring from the body
of African traditional society. Thus he found it easy to
convince himself that the Akida system represented the worst
features of Arab and German domination of the African people.
He refused to believe that there did not exist under the
layers of foreign inspired bureaucracy a kernel of the older
system which could be nurtured into a better form of government. Sir Donald was, therefore, willing to sanction the
brief imposition of his type of indirect rule because it
held out the possibility of rebuilding the older forms.

By the end of 1926, despite all the difficulties, the
new Native Authorities were functioning throughout Tanganyika, and Cameron could begin to make alterations to improve
the system. The Native Courts were an obvious target for
reform. They were administratively subordinate to the ordinary courts of Tanganyika, and appeals against decisions of
a Native Court could be taken to the High Court of the territory. Cameron believed that there could be no healthy
development of the African courts as long as they were
dominated by an alien judicial system. The administration
of justice, as a rule, had been but another side of the coin
to the executive and legislative functions of African leaders.
The German and British systems had forced a separation of
these two powers.

Sir Donald proposed to remove the African courts in almost all cases from the jurisdiction of the High Court. He
wanted supervision and control over the African courts to be
vested in the hands of administrators. The Native Authority
Ordinance of 1926 had in theory withdrawn from the district
officers some of their potential for direct interference in

80

the affairs of the Native Authorities. Nevertheless, Cameron believed that the district officers were in a better position to supervise the Native Courts than were the judges of the ordinary courts. Sir Alison Russell, Chief Justice of Tanganyika, disagreed vehemently with Cameron's ideas. He pressed his arguments for the separation of powers on the home government. Eventually the Colonial Office was called upon to choose between Cameron's proposals and Russell's arguments, and Amery finally supported Cameron's position.[30] The Native Courts Ordinance of 1929 put into effect Cameron's concepts of African law. The ordinance even prevented African barristers from appearing for clients except in non-Native Courts. In this, Cameron's reasoning was impeccable, although it can in retrospect be considered shortsighted. Native Courts were for the traditional African and the concept of Western educated barristers representing clients was foreign to any traditional system.

Cameron's attitude toward African education was in keeping with the changes he had made in the other areas of life in Tanganyika. The educational system he inherited from Governor Byatt was just beginning to recover from the disastrous war years. At the end of World War I the German Lutheran missions which had provided the bulk of African education under German rule were turned over to allied or neutral groups. The Wesleyans and Church of Scotland missionaries were placed in general charge of such stations. This state of affairs prevailed until 1925 when the stations were finally returned to their former owners. The unsettled nature of tenure hampered any major church plans for improving African education. There was also no system of giving government grants-in-aid to church schools until Dr. Oldham and Ormsby-Gore agreed upon a code for Tanganyika. The government in 1920 created a Department of Education and appointed Stanley Rivers-Smith, an energetic, able man, as its head, but he was handicapped in the early years by a lack of funds and personnel. He spent much of his time in the first years trying to trace down educated Africans in order to build the nucleus of a teaching staff. In 1922 there were only two European teachers active in the government schools in the entire territory. However, in the next eight years the educational system of Tanganyika grew tremendously as a result of the work of dedicated teachers, district officers, and African chiefs. In Sir Donald the educators found a man who understood the need for educating the younger generation of Africans and who gave their proposed programs his personal encouragement; even more important, he diverted an ever increasing amount of money to education. The following table shows the extent of this monetary support.[31]

Year	Total tax revenue	Total expenditure on education	Percent of total revenue
1924-25	£1,324,670	£ 15,754	1.18
1925-26	1,975,400	24,491	1.44
1926-27	2,202,908	45,923	2.08
1927-28	2,486,278	59,692	3.21
1928-29	1,972,858	75,947	3.85
1929-30	1,992,675	89,829	4.50
1930-31	1,749,478	111,302	6.36
1931-32	1,522,368	122,666	8.06

The sixfold increase in educational revenues between 1924 and
1932 was lost during the depression era when the education
budget fell to only 3.83 percent of total revenues in 1936.
    Tanganyika's educational system as developed under
Cameron can be considered under three separate but interlocking divisions--the mission schools, educational facilities
for the sons of chiefs, and village or Native Authority
schools. When Sir Donald arrived in Tanganyika he discovered
that Byatt's government had ignored the mission schools.
Cameron believed that this was shortsighted since it cost
roughly twice as much to operate a government school as a
mission school. Therefore, in 1925 Cameron invited the
missions to take over the bulk of education in the territory
and promised that the government would support the undertaking
with grants on the basis of the Grant-in-Aid Code of the
Education Department.[32] The result of this cooperation was
immediately apparent as the missions opened dozens of new
schools throughout the territory. Most of these were elementary schools which tended to stress very basic academic
knowledge and industrial crafts. Until 1927 the Protestant
missions took the lead in educating African children, with
minimum proselytizing. In that year the Catholic Church
announced that its missionaries, too, should stress education
over evangelism.
    The second category, education for the sons and heirs
of chiefs, is largely related to the establishment of the
Tabora Government School. The district officer there in 1922
had taken over the old school building for use as a hospital.
Subsequently a new school was built two miles out of town.
The Superintendent of Education for Tabora Province, A.
Travers Lacey, suggested converting this into a boarding
school for the sons of chiefs. Cameron approved the proposal
and budgeted £20,000 for the construction of facilities for
180 boys. Long before Sir Donald laid the foundation stone
for the permanent buildings in 1928, there were students in

the school. The first pupils entered in February 1925. They had been selected after the education officers and district officers had combed the village schools for talented boys related to the ruling classes. The three Rs were stressed in the first four forms, with instruction in Swahili. Advanced classes consisted of traditional academic instruction and vocational training. Some observers have argued that the Tabora School was Cameron's most lasting contribution since many of Tanganyika's leaders over the past two generations have been educated there.

The third type of school developed while Cameron was governor was the village or Native Authority school. Village schools were maintained in some of the larger villages and stressed the most elementary type of instruction. Rivers-Smith had made Swahili instead of the local languages the lingua franca for instruction on the lower levels throughout Tanganyika, and this was the language used in the village schools. Cecil McMahon, the District Officer of Shinyanga in Mwanza Province, with the cooperation of the Sukuma chiefs and Cameron's enthusiastic approval, began the first Native Authority boarding school for children of commoners. The instruction in these schools was also a blend of academic and vocational work. The first government boarding school for girls was also begun during Cameron's administration. It was an elementary school founded at Tabora in 1929.[33]

Tanganyika's system of education measured by Western standards was, even in the 1950s, inadequate. It is, however, difficult not to applaud Sir Donald's contributions to the establishment of a firm beginning for the education of Tanganyika's Africans. He did not, it is true, generate the new ideas for educational development himself. Men such as the head of the Education Department, Stanley Rivers-Smith, his deputy, A. A. Isherwood, and concerned district officers like McMahon had the specific ideas for change. But Cameron made certain that these ideas could be put into effect.

Within four years of his arrival Cameron had completely revitalized every aspect of administration in Tanganyika. He had carried the day in his protracted debate with Amery and Grigg over closer union. Central and district government efficiency had been greatly increased largely because of new procedures established by the governor. The Native Authority system was functioning even in those areas where it was merely the result of a British creation of what was imagined to be traditional authority. Cameron's reforms had caught the imagination of almost all qualified observers. The distinguished historian, Dame Margery Perham, remembers how kind

and helpful Cameron was to her when she stopped in Tanganyika
during her first prolonged tour of Africa. He arranged for
her to visit the interior and gave her a relatively free hand
to go anywhere and ask all kinds of questions. She left Tanganyika very deeply impressed by what Cameron had accomplished.[34]

Official opinion was just as favorable as that of Dame
Margery. Cameron had always believed that there was no conflict between the highest ideals of British government and
the terms of the mandate, and the Permanent Mandates Commission had by 1929 come to support fully his reforms in Tanganyika. When Cameron left the territory the Commission
openly praised his policies while expressing the hope that
subsequent governors would not change them. Cameron's support in Britain during the waning days of the closer union
imbroglio indicated how men such as Ramsay MacDonald, J. H.
Thomas, and Sidney Webb viewed his tenure of office. The
British government's position toward Cameron was most posi-
tively stated by the Earl of Plymouth, Parliamentary undersecretary of the Colonial Office, in testimony to the Permanent Mandates Commission after Cameron had been Governor
of Nigeria for over a year. He reported that the further
development of the system of self-government begun by Sir
Donald in Tanganyika was among "the most important and the
most fascinating of the tasks which lie before the British
Colonial Administration."[35]

In summing up Cameron's achievement in Tanganyika one
must be careful not to allow the justifiable accolades to
obscure certain facts. For instance, there is a tendency to
suppose that Cameron created a decentralized type of administration. It was far from that. On his arrival in Tanganyika, Cameron had looked carefully at the central and local
government structure and found an ad hoc system operating.
The potential power of the governor was greatly modified by
his having to operate through an archaic system. Cameron
was above all else a brilliant administrator and the first
moves he made were to strengthen the position of the central
administration. Even the creation of the Legislative Council
can be viewed as an act that would give more support to the
governor's decisions. Without minimizing in the slightest
Cameron's motivation to safeguard the interests of the
Africans, one can still say that the changes in the Native
Authority system enhanced the direct influence of the European officers in the field. By giving back to African rulers
a modicum of their traditional authority, the governor made
them more receptive to direction from above. By having central government edicts or even the wishes of the governor

conveyed to the people by leaders of their own choosing, he removed much of the sting from unpopular measures. Thus, there existed in Tanganyika in 1930 a seeming paradox. Cameron had succeeded in restoring a large proportion of local government decision making to the African, while at the same time he had increased the degree of central control over their lives.

In retrospect, Cameron's major failing in Tanganyika was but a reflection of that of the British throughout their African dependent empire. Few persons in decision-making positions either in Whitehall or in Africa ever planned policies teleologically. British administration at its best was a marvel of pragmatism, and Cameron was a master at creating administrative structures to solve specific short-term problems. But did he have a vision of Tanganyika's future and were his policies designed to secure that future? The tentative reply to this question seems to be that Cameron had first asked himself "To what end is my administration working?", and had then arrived at some general ideas concerning the future political development of the territory.

Sir Donald was aware of the deficiencies in the Native Authority system he had sponsored, but he believed that time, hard work, and close cooperation between the administration and the African people would bring about improvements in the system. This process of change was applauded by Sir Donald because to him the greatest threat to improvement was that his system would become static. If Native Administrations were not constantly revised to accommodate the progressive development of the people, the government would then be responsible for creating nothing but a human zoo.[36] As more Africans were educated, councils would be expanded to make room for their representatives, for Cameron knew that the educated elite would not long remain subservient to ignorant traditional leaders. Cameron was aware that in time the powers of the chiefs would have to be greatly modified. Time again was the prime factor in the consolidation of many of the fragmented Native Authorities into fewer large and more affluent government units. By the time Sir Donald left Tanganyika tribal councils of this type were already well developed in the Bukoba and Mwanza districts.

Cameron was vehement in his opposition to any attempts to introduce Western style democracy, complete with the ballot box, to Tanganyika. He wrote later in defense of his policy that if he had attempted to base his political reforms on English institutions he would have "created political chaos and anarchy where some order previously existed, with no compensating advantage to the individuals concerned.

Society, for the present, is from this point of view of much more importance than the individuals who make up that society and to have bestowed 'votes' on the latter at once, would, I believe, have been as useful to them and their society as if we had given them toy balloons or neopolitan ices."[37]

In his testimony to the Parliamentary Joint Committee, Cameron expressed his belief that the future would see a gradual development of the Native Authority system toward a series of interdependent regional and central councils. The first step should be the creation of regional councils where chiefs from a given area could meet to discuss common problems. The second phase would see the establishment of a central native council which would consider all matters of importance to the Africans throughout the territory. This central council would choose delegates to meet representatives of a non-African council, and such joint meetings would take over from the presently constituted Legislative Council. Representatives on the regional councils would probably be selected by a combination of modified traditional and Western methods. As the electorate became more educated and gained more experience, it could be given more responsibility. In this rather indefinite view of the future Cameron always implied that Britain would have a direct role in the government of the territory.[38]

6

Nigerian Developments, 1924-1931

Sir Donald Cameron indicated in his memoirs that he had welcomed the end of his tenure as Governor of Tanganyika. He was fifty-eight years old and had been in charge of one of the most difficult territories in the British dependent empire for almost six years. In that time he had traveled to almost every part of Tanganyika, had completely reorganized the Native Authority system, restored the economic well-being of the people, and successfully resisted the attempt of his superiors to join Tanganyika to its northern neighbors. He was close to physical collapse, and it is obvious that Lady Cameron whose health was never robust also needed a long rest. Cameron informed the Colonial Office in mid-1930 that he planned to leave Tanganyika the following January. Lord Passfield, however, facing the first tremors of the world-wide depression, did not wish to see Cameron retire, and he asked him to remain as governor for an indefinite period until the Parliamentary Joint Committee had completed its work. Cameron demurred and stated that he would stay only if it was announced publicly that he did so at the specific request of His Majesty's government.

The Colonial Office shortly informed Cameron that he could return home as originally planned. This was soon followed by a semi-official letter which must have contained a reprimand for his attitude. He later remarked that after this communication he believed he had little chance of further employment. Thus he was very surprised when he received a telegram from Passfield in December offering him the position of Governor of Nigeria.[1] He was eager to accept this appointment because in its way it provided as much of a challenge as had Tanganyika in 1925. Cameron therefore had the satisfaction of knowing before he left Tanganyika that he was going to have an opportunity to put his ideas to work in Nigeria, an area where he had spent so much of his life in subordinate posts.

In January 1931, Cameron addressed the Tanganyika Legislative Council for the last time. A part of that speech is worth quoting at length since it indicates not only his attitude toward his work, but also much of Cameron's personality.

There are a great many estimable people, many of whom I know and admire who would take this opportunity to deliver a long funeral oration on their own official corpse. Such a thing is quite foreign to my nature. If I have achieved anything in this country I have achieved it with the assistance of others, officials and unofficials, not the least in this Council, and I do not claim the credit or desire it. If anything has been done that is of value it will speak for it-self. No word that I can utter can lend any value or add any value to any of the acts of the Administration during the last six years. If the work has been good it will endure, until, of course, by the modification of circumstances some adjustment will be necessary, as will be inevitable.[2]

This was not an attempt at false modesty, but an example of Cameron's ability to look at himself and his work with cold objectivity.

Despite Cameron's expressed desires, his leave-taking from Tanganyika was charged with emotion. Members of the administrative service subscribed a considerable sum on their own initiative to have the governor's portrait painted. They wanted it to be presented either to Lady Cameron or to the Tanganyika government. The Colonial Office, however, vetoed both schemes, and the money was eventually given to the new Anglican Church at Dar es Salaam for a carved pulpit and reading desk.[3] There were also spontaneous demonstrations of appreciation from chiefs and headmen from all over Tanganyika. Large numbers came to Dar es Salaam at their own expense to meet the governor and bid him goodbye. A large delegation came from Bukoba where Cameron's policy had thwarted the ambitions of the traditional rulers more than in any other area. After receiving them, he tried to persuade them not to wait for his departure but to leave the heat and humidity of Dar es Salaam and go home. But the chiefs informed him that they had come of their own accord because that was what their people wanted and if they left before the governor sailed, their people would be ashamed.[4] Perhaps the most moving farewell to Cameron was sent by a chief of a distant area who asked the district officer to

Tell him we do not wish him to go. We hope he will not forget us. We shall not forget him. He has done much for us. Our children will not forget him; nor yet their children.[5]

With the last farewells said, Governor and Lady Cameron sailed from Dar es Salaam on 1 February 1931. They were never to return.

Soon after arriving in England Cameron was called upon
to give evidence before the Parliamentary Joint Committee.
He was in very poor health and the demands of appearing before the committee proved too much. Two days after he had
finished testifying he collapsed and was ordered to the
south coast for a long period of rest and recuperation.
Rumors reached Nigeria that Cameron had died, and this added
to the confusion in that administration.[6] Freedom from the
killing schedule of work that Cameron had imposed on himself
and the sea air worked wonders, and Sir Donald had almost
recovered his health when he arrived in Nigeria in June 1931.

No direct evidence exists to indicate why Lord Passfield,
who was more than slightly disturbed by Cameron in July 1930,
changed his attitude toward him by December. It seems obvious, however, that the Colonial Office finally realized
how serious were the errors of Governor Thomson's administration. The women's disturbances showed clearly how potentially explosive the situation was in all southern Nigeria.
Thomson was a sick man, the morale of the Nigerian service
was low, law and order were still being maintained by the
army and the police in large areas of the protectorate, and
the world depression was worsening. If Cameron, who had
an impeccable record as an administrator, could be persuaded
to return to Nigeria, then Passfield could consider that he
had made a significant first step in solving the manifold
problems of that troubled area. Nigeria presented an irresis-
tible challenge to Cameron. He had served there under three
governors and had disagreed vehemently with many of the implications of the policies of Lord Lugard, the most dominant of
these personalities. As governor, even in depression times,
he would have the opportunity of correcting not just the
short-range disarrangements, but also the long-term policies
of the protectorate.

The immediate problems confronting Cameron in June 1931,
however varied, could be grouped into two major categories--
those that concerned the southern areas and those that per-
tained to northern Nigeria. Of the two groups, those relating to southeastern Nigeria were of the most pressing concern. Sir Hugh Clifford had managed to avoid extending
direct taxation to those territories and had left his successor to deal with Colonial Office and Nigerian bureaucratic
pressure to tidy up the administrative service. Governor
Clifford was too intelligent and experienced not to see the
dangers of forcing conformity on the eastern provinces merely
for the sake of standardization. Even the proponents of taxing the Ibo and Ibibio people admitted that the tax was not
designed to bring in revenue, but to bring the East in line
with administrative practices elsewhere.

89

Graeme Thomson, who became Governor of Nigeria in 1925, had no previous experience in Africa. He came to the Colonial Service very late, having distinguished himself in administration in Britain first at the Admiralty and then in Transport. He began his colonial career as the Colonial Secretary of Ceylon in 1919 and in the following year was made the Governor of Guiana. In retrospect, there were a number of factors that worked against Thomson in Nigeria. One was his lack of experience in the governance of alien people. After only six years, all at the upper levels of government, he was given one of the most prestigious posts in the Colonial Service. The position he held and his tendency toward impetuousity and over confidence also contributed to Thomson's failures. A governor of a British territory was almost a law unto himself, the only checks upon him being the Colonial Office and his own sense of proportion. Most successful governors surrounded themselves with an able staff and sought advice from a variety of sources before making major decisions. A few days after his arrival in November 1925, Thomson, new to Nigeria and for that matter Africa, believed himself well enough informed to make a decision which Clifford had postponed for years and with which the majority of the field staff in the East disagreed. He decided to extend taxation to the eastern areas.

In December 1925, the Residents and district officers were informed of the imminence of taxation and were invited to comment on the central government's decision. Almost all of their replies were guardedly pessimistic. None wanted to appear to oppose the entire project outright. Most, however, wanted the government to undertake detailed surveys of the political, social, and economic bases of the societies before deciding on a specific plan. They also urged a go-slow policy in establishing whatever system was decided upon. The time requested for installing the new system varied from one district to another, but many believed that the assessment registers would take at least a year to complete. Many Residents such as F. B. Adams of Owerri Province and P. Amaury Talbot of Warri Province requested that the police force be substantially strengthened before any attempts were made to collect the tax.[7]

The Lieutenant-Governor of the Southern Provinces, Major U. F. Ruxton, worked throughout the summer of 1926 on the draft proposal for a new tax ordinance. Because of his considerable knowledge of the eastern areas, Ruxton wanted to keep the assessment policies and actual taxing plan as simple as possible. Eventually he proposed a capitation tax on every male above the age of sixteen. Such a tax would have the advantage of keeping assessment officers in the areas for a minimum amount of time, and it was hoped that this would arouse fewer suspicions among the Ibo, Ibibio, and Ijaw people. Thus the detested Warrant Chiefs would be kept in the background.[8] Unfortunately Ruxton's plans were not accepted by the government. The Lieutenant-Governor of the Northern Provinces, H. Richmond Palmer, and the Resident at Kano, C. W. Alexander, both demurred.[9] They felt that there should be a standard tax system throughout Nigeria and that the chiefs should be the main focal point for this system. District officers should be kept as far as possible in the background. Naturally these officials believed the northern system should be applied to the East as it had earlier been extended to the West. In this opinion they were joined by G. J. F. Tomlinson, the Secretary for Native Affairs, who complained that Ruxton's draft was too literally "adapted to the facts as they exist today"; he recommended that the government "indulge in a little make believe" in regard to the establishment of Native Treasuries in the East.[10] Thomson, confronted with the opposition of the northerners, decided against Ruxton's pragmatic approach and ordered in March 1927 that the Native Revenue Ordinance of 1917 which had applied the tax system to most of southern Nigeria be amended to include the five eastern provinces.[11]

The field staff was notified that Native Treasuries, based upon the Native Court areas, were to be established by 1 October 1927. Taxation would be introduced officially on 1 April 1928.[12] In this interim period district officers were to make detailed assessment reports on every family in every village in their areas. They were also to ascertain the wealth of all adult males so that a fair average income could be established. The theoretical tax rate would then be applied as 2.5 percent of a man's projected income. District officers throughout the eastern provinces did heroic work trying to comply with their orders. Some of the assessment reports were models of anthropological inquiry and these gave the central authorities, for the first time in over thirty years, detailed and accurate data on the people of the East. Unfortunately the emphasis was upon economics, and district officers, pressed for time and facing the open and covert hostility of the people, used a number of questionable expedients in arriving at the taxable wealth of the men in their districts.[13] These included counting yam hills in a small area and then projecting this number for a larger acreage and guessing at "average" yields of yams, maize, and corn. The same procedure was followed in estimating the number of oil palm trees. The district officers also did not have the time or the knowledge to make a distinction between produce consumed and produce sold. Thus it is not surprising that most

district officers found the taxable wealth of their areas
to be the same as that figure suggested by the government
before the assessments. Except in rare instances, the tax
rate for the East became seven shillings per adult male.[14]

Tax collection began almost immediately in April 1928
and was completed by June. There was no standard method of
collecting the money; the Warrant Chiefs as well as the
traditional rulers were used by the government to get the
villagers to pay. Despite the difficulties of collecting
the tax and the threat of non-cooperation in a few areas,
the collection proceeded smoothly. A total of £364,824 was
collected, and in most cases 50 percent was rebated to the
districts to be used for the salaries of local government
officials and the construction of new offices and council
houses for the Native Administration.[15] The collection of
the tax in 1929 reconfirmed the central government's quiet
assurance that its policies were correct. Even less opposition against the tax was recorded and £324,690 was collected.[16] Governor Thomson's advisors must have congratulated
themselves on paying no attention to what seemed the over-
emotional warnings by district officers of violent reactions.

The entire superstructure of "traditional" government
in the East, so carefully constructed by Lugard and his successors, was brought down by the actions of a normally quies-
cent sector of African societies. The women in Owerri and
Calabar Provinces had watched their men being taxed at a
time when the declining market value for produce had reduced
the amount of money in circulation. New customs and market
regulations also portended for them further detrimental
changes in the eastern economy. Reassessments begun inno-
cently by inexperienced district officers in both provinces
gave credence to rumors that the government was going to
begin taxing women. On 23 November 1929, the women's organizations at Oloko were informed of a quarrel between an African assessment agent and a woman over his attempt to recount
her husband's assets. They considered this certain proof of
the government's intention to tax women. Within three days
over 2500 women had gathered at Oloko in the immediate vicinity of the Warrant Chief's house. Their objective soon
became more than a guarantee from the district officer that
they would not be taxed. They intimidated him so much that
he dismissed the Warrant Chief from office and held him for
trial on charges made by the women.[17]

The news of the success of the Oloko protest spread
rapidly throughout the East, and other women joined in trying to rid themselves of the Warrant Chiefs. The actions
were the same everywhere. Women in great numbers congregated

near the Native Court buildings and demanded that the British remove the offending official. An accident to a woman at Aba in early December caused women for the first time to become violent and resulted in some burning and looting.[18] After this incident, women not only intimidated the Warrant Chiefs but also burned many Native Court buildings. The government at first was not prepared to cope with such seemingly spontaneous occurrences, but it soon rushed regular police, reserve police, and military units to the affected areas. By early December, when the disturbances had become widespread in Calabar Province, large numbers of troops had been mobilized to contain the movement. At Abak on 14 December, soldiers fired on a mass of women and killed three. The next day at Utu-Etim-Ekpo troops again clashed with a large crowd of women with dreadful results. Eighteen women were killed and nineteen wounded. On 16 December an even larger number of women were driven from Opobo by point-blank firing into the threatening crowd. Twenty six women were killed immediately and thirty-one wounded.[19]

The use of firearms against large crowds of women who believed themselves protected from such violence halted the women's disturbances, which had spread quickly throughout the two provinces when it appeared that the government would give way to their demands to stop reassessment and to remove unpopular Warrant Chiefs. The appalling loss of life, however reprehensible, appears in retrospect to have been the major factor in keeping the eastern government from a complete collapse, since the women's protests died away almost as rapidly as they had begun. It was not possible for the Nigerian central authorities to hide from the Colonial Office and Parliament the riotous behavior of thousands of women and the deaths of almost fifty by the rifle fire of soldiers. Lord Passfield's suspicions of the competence of the Nigerian central government had become by early 1930 an established bloody fact.[20] Obviously something had to be done to maintain law and order in the East. Columns of soldiers and police operating under the Peace Preservation Ordinance could halt the immediate threat of further demonstrations, but could not guarantee long-range stability.[21] Complete reordering of the method of government to meet more adequately the needs of the people was imperative. This demand in all probability was the main reason why Lord Passfield decided in late 1930 to offer the post of Governor of Nigeria to Cameron.

The primarily Yoruba areas of western Nigeria presented the new governor with problems that were far less acute. They were rather the continuation of those created during Lugard's administration and perpetuated by his successors. At Oyo and Abeokuta there still remained the scars of the

disturbances of a decade and a half before. In all the Native
Authority areas the chiefs had been given more power than
they had traditionally possessed, and one of the major tasks
of the British field officers had become the securing of
peaceful adherence of Yoruba groups to the new and greater
authority of their chiefs. There were also a number of areas
where the Native Authority boundaries needed to be redrawn.
A prime example of this problem was Ibadan, the largest city
in Nigeria and by the 1920s the center of Westernized activity
in Yorubaland. Yet Ibadan was still subservient to the
authority of the Alafin of Oyo.[22]

Developments in Lagos, while they might be purely urban,
had a tendency to affect the western areas much more than any
other section of Nigeria. The most serious general question
that agitated Lagos in the 1920s concerned the role of educated Nigerians in the present and future political system
of Nigeria. All senior administrators, Cameron included, were
suspicious of the motives of the educated "elite." Tied as
they were to some concept of traditional rule, the British
could not envision an African political system that was not
dominated by chiefs or traditional rulers. The standard
answer given to the key question of how these traditional
authorities could be reshaped according to Western models
was that the chiefs or their sons had to be educated. Missionaries, who had been active in southern Nigeria for almost a hundred years, had done their work well by educating
large numbers of Nigerians. In the 1920s in all the larger
cities there were a significant number of university trained
Nigerians. But such men were systematically excluded from
the governance of their country unless they could become a
member of a traditional ruling clique. Nigerian lawyers
could not even represent a client in a Native Authority Court.
The British excused this provision by saying they were protecting the gullible African from being cheated. To a Nigerian lawyer this was not only a flimsy, but an insulting, excuse. The only places where Westernized Nigerians could
participate in governing their country were on a few town
councils, notably Lagos, and after 1923 on the Legislative
Council.

Although in retrospect one can see the educated Nigerians as the wave of the future, the British viewed many of
them as nothing but troublemakers whose actions too often
depended upon advancing themselves. It is not surprising,
therefore, that all governors of Nigeria kept a close check
on the political activities of such men as Herbert Macauley
whose Lagos based political party, the National Democratic
Party, held all the elective seats on the Legislative Council.
Macaulay was one of the most vehement defenders of Eshugbayi,

the Eleko of Lagos, who had been removed from office for not cooperating with the British local authorities. Far from helping his cause, Macaulay's statements in London had merely convinced Cameron, who was acting governor in 1920, to cancel Eshugbayi's right to act as hereditary ruler of Lagos.[23] In the 1920s and early 1930s Macaulay kept this and other local issues alive in Lagos, and they spilled over into the neighboring Yoruba hinterland. However, the government had contained the activities of the few Nigerian nationalists very successfully, and although they could prove embarrassing, they were never a danger to the continuance of a given policy.[24]

The problems in the North were of a different order. Northern Nigeria was considered by many colonial experts to be the "quintessence" of excellent administration. This area had been Lugard's canvas on which he had created in bold outlines those principles of indirect rule that lesser men had been only too grateful to follow. To a conservative Colonial Office, the long established civilized rule of the emirs provided just the kind of peace and good order that it wished for all the territories under its control. The men who were selected to aid the Muslim rulers in governing their areas tended to admire Muslim society before being posted to the North or else soon became converts to the northern system. Men such as C. W. Alexander and H. Richmond Palmer immersed themselves in the intricacies of northern culture and government, particularly as represented by the Hausa-Fulani. Most of the northern administrators were incapable of suggesting any substantial reforms of the system. This was either because they could genuinely say in the manner of the Duke of Wellington that what was represented was the best system possible or because as junior officers they had no intention of jeopardizing their careers by attacking the decisions of their superiors.

The northern administrators did not welcome what they considered to be unwarranted criticism from the central Secretariat in Lagos. Sir Hugh Clifford had isolated some of the major weaknesses of British rule in the North, but his reports were considered by his superiors to be evidence of jealousy toward Lugard, and he was unable to accomplish any significant change. Sir Graeme Thomson did not have sufficient experience in governing Muslim territories to know if anything was wrong in the North. In addition he was ill throughout much of his tenure of office. He tended therefore to allow the northern lieutenant-governor and the Residents to have their head. Thus the errors noted by Clifford in 1922 went unchecked for a decade, and contrary to the expressed wishes of Lugard, the system of indirect rule in predominantly Muslim areas became static.[25] In non-

Muslim or so-called pagan areas little was done to correct erroneous boundaries, discover the traditional rulers, or relieve the people from the sometimes oppressive and almost always foreign control by the Hausa-Fulani.

Many European officers posted to the Muslim emirates soon came to admire individual rulers and the system that produced such a well-ordered society. Bolstered by Lugard's precepts, while in some cases completely misunderstanding them, Europeans allowed many of the emirs to become almost independent of central control. As Margery Perham noted after her visits to Nigeria in the 1930s, the tendency in the North was to view the world totally from the standpoint of the Native Authorities. If a Resident had learned his lessons of indirect rule too well, he would regard the intrusion of Western government practices or education as a retrograde step and an unwarranted disturbance of the status quo.[26]

Most northern officials in responsible positions in the 1920s treated the emirates as if they were similar to the princely states in India instead of being transitional, pragmatic conveniences. Compounding the problem was the attitude held by many Europeans that southern Nigeria was populated by a bewildering number of restless people, all of whom represented lesser cultures than those of the Hausa-Fulani and Kanuri. Northern officers did not wish to look to the South for examples. They also considered the central government at Lagos to be filled by men with no direct field experience and who were out of touch with reality.

Residents in the larger emirates tended to avoid any show of direct authority. In the best tradition of Indian administration, they preferred to wield power from behind a veil. Their working relations with the emirs and the high officers of a Native Administration depended upon a complicated balance between the acceptance on both sides of where ultimate authority resided and how far the Resident would go in any given case in asserting that authority. The greater the authority of the Muslim ruler, the greater the potential influence of the advisor. Many Residents, however, instead of using this latent power to effect slow but progressive change in economic and social affairs, on the contrary intrenched their position until they were more conservative than the emirs.[27]

In contrast to other British territories there was an excellent tax rebate system for the northern areas. After 1928 the emirates with fully organized Native Treasuries were allowed to keep 70 percent of the direct taxes collected in their area. The following table gives the basic data for the five largest northern emirates.[28]

Emirate	Population	Area in square miles	Revenue 1932-33 (£)
Kano	1,992,263	12,217	233,114
Sokoto	1,323,531	25,608	121,679
Katsina	925,360	8,490	86,845
Bornu	433,121	33,159	70,174
Adamawa	403,110	19,944	32,820

The picture of a series of prosperous emirates is somewhat
modified when one considers that over 75 percent of expenditure in the North went on general administration costs and
recurrent expenses. Only 4.3 percent was spent on education,
4.1 percent on medical services, 8 percent on capital outlay,
and only 0.5 percent on agriculture.[29] Thus the greatest
beneficiaries of the Native Treasury system were the emirs
and the Native Authority staff.

The very real danger inherent in the practice of British
administration in the northern Muslim areas was the creation
of de facto rival polities operating within the theoretical
context of a united Nigeria. Before the British conquest of
the North, there had been a definite unity throughout the
Hausa-Fulani areas. Although practically free from outside
control in mundane affairs, each emir owed allegiance to the
Sultan of Sokoto. This fact combined with the powers of his
nobles and his council, and ultimately the fear of assassina-
tion or deposition, kept most of the emirate governments from
becoming too despotic, and in the century after Usuman dan
Fodio a loose but nevertheless real unity had been maintained
in the North.[30] The British conquest loosened the ties with
Sokoto, and the actions of the Residents in the 1920s in viewing the emirates as separate entities threatened even further
the slim bonds of traditional political cooperation between
them.

One problem which Lugard had imagined he had settled
was the relationship between administrative officers and
representatives of departments such as Agriculture, Public
Works, etc. He had made it clear that department officers
were subordinate to the Residents and should be guided by
their instructions unless these were openly incompatible
with orders from the director of the department in Lagos.
Their approach to the Native Authority had to be through
the Residents. Although Lugard had insisted upon the necessity for close cooperation, it had been necessary for Clifford to restate the position in 1920, and in 1926 Clifford's
memorandum on this subject was again reissued. He admonished
the department heads to relinquish some of their direct control and give the departmental officers in the field more

discretion to cooperate with their political counterparts. Despite the efforts of the central government to control the situation, there had continued to develop a schismatic movement in the North where there was a rigid severence between political and non-political officers. By the close of the 1920s this had created a near paralysis of vital services by some departments in parts of the North.[31] There was hostility and suspicion between the two branches. This complicated further the already unhealthy divided political situation.

The greatest anomaly in governing the North noted by Sir Hugh Clifford in his correspondence with the Colonial Office was in the so-called pagan areas. The whole thrust of Lugard's system of indirect rule had rested upon the assumption that the people were being ruled, in some fashion, by their traditional leaders. But it was obvious in the early 1920s that many non-Muslim peoples were being forced to accept aliens as rulers. These foreigners, most notably the Fulani, had been attempting to secure control over some of these pagan territories for over a century. Even where the British had not used Muslim chiefs in pagan areas, they had introduced the district system which had no counterpart in the traditional forms of rule. Thus many of the less developed northern clans had been forced to comply with a governmental system at variance with their institutions, as had the Ibo and Ibibio. A brief glance at the most important pagan areas will indicate the degree to which the northern administration after Lugard had allowed this system to develop.

Southern Zaria Emirate was largely inhabited by non-Muslim people. They were administered by district heads, usually Fulani, who did not understand the languages of those they ruled and did not care for the customs of the people. This area was far from district headquarters and was not well supervised by the British administrative officers. Further to the northeast in the Plateau and Bauchi Provinces were the Plateau tribes comprising over thirty different groups of people. Many of these groups felt they had not been conquered and were a continual source of trouble to the administration. As late as 1930 a district officer had been stoned to death by a group from one of these tribes. In general, Britain attempted to rule on the Plateau by means of dummy traditional authorities similar in form to those which caused the uprisings in southern Nigeria. Many of the district heads appointed over the Plateau tribes were Hausa who did not like or appreciate their charges. The threat of immediate British police action, however, tended to keep violence at a minimum.[32] Further to the east in Dikwa Emirate the hill people had never been subdued by the Muslim armies of the Shehu of Dikwa. British military sweeps through the country in the first two decades of the twentieth century had, however, brought a reluctant acceptance of British and Muslim rule. British policy from the very beginning had aimed at forcing the pagan groups to accept the overlordship of the Shehu. Alien district heads were tolerated and there was no representative from these territories on the Shehu's council.[33]

The situation in Benue Province among the Tiv was reminiscent of the Ibo areas to the south. The 600,000 Tiv had traditionally been organized into more than thirty clans. They were extremely proud, fierce people who had successfully resisted the military intrusions of foreigners until the coming of British troops. As late as 1923 British administrators always traveled in Tiv territory with a military escort. The district system was applied to the Tiv, and since no real attempt was made to understand the complexity of Tiv institutions, the British tended to appoint the wrong people, generally young men, to act as district heads. Beneath the facade of indirect rule the traditional Tiv clan government continued to function, although it was seriously handicapped by having little support from the Residents and district officers.[34]

Conditions among the 150,000 Igala were considerably worse than even those of the Tiv. When the British occupation became effective, their kingdom was divided between the Protectorates of Northern and Southern Nigeria, and this situation remained unchanged even after amalgamation. The Atta, the traditional ruler, was located at Idah in the South, while his territories in the North were further divided between the two provinces of Benue and Plateau and three divisions. At first the British believed they could make indirect rule function among the Igala in the North by using subordinate authorities and ignoring the Atta. Subsequently, minor boundary reorganizations were undertaken in 1918 and 1921, and in 1926 the territorial integrity of the kingdom was almost completely restored. However, the traditional government was still operated by district heads rather than officials appointed by the Atta, and the Atta's council was not allowed to function.[35]

It is clear that the Nigeria to which Cameron returned in 1931 was much more unhealthy than when he had left six years before. Old wrongs had remained while new ones had been added. Traditional government structures throughout much of Nigeria, which had been ignored during the early years of the occupation, continued to suffer. The southeast, so recently the scene of riots and conflict, still required policing by constables and army units; the political situation

there was chaotic. Only in the North did the central authorities have a good understanding of the traditional customs
and practices of the people. Unfortunately undue deference
to the northern emirs was threatening to create a state within a state. Already many British administrators in the North
felt they were above obeying directly the orders of the central authorities.

Overshadowing all the questions of government reorganization and economic development was the deepening depression.
The lowering of prices for primary products combined with new
customs duties on key imports had been one of the contributory
causes for the women's disturbances. By the time Cameron
arrived in Nigeria, the projected emergency budget for the
year 1931-32 had already been stringently revised downward.
Cameron had confronted the beginnings of the economic depression before he left Tanganyika, but even he could have no idea
of how much time and effort would be required in order to
keep Nigeria solvent. This salient fact should be kept in
mind when assessing Cameron's successes or failures as Governor of Nigeria. He was never a free agent who could use the
bulk of his time wrestling with the problems of administration and applying vigorously the remedies he believed best.
In the four years after his arrival, any reforms he made in
the archaic system he inherited from Graeme Thomson had to
be achieved with a steadily declining operating budget.

7

The Nigerian Financial Crisis

Soon after Sir Donald Cameron arrived in Nigeria he was
visited by Dame Margery Perham who was just beginning an exhaustive research tour of the territory. Once again as in
Tanganyika she found Cameron willing to devote his time and
energies to clearing the way for her trek into the interior.
Since she stayed at Government House, she was able to have a
number of conversations with Cameron in which he discussed
at great length his views of Nigeria's problems. He had completely recovered from his physical collapse and was ebul-
lient and optimistic about the future. He appeared to enjoy
the tremendous challenge of reorienting the disastrous government policies in the East and redirecting the Native Authority
system in the North.[1] Although Cameron was able in the four
years of his administration to alter some of the policies of
his predecessors and to evolve new Native Authority and Native
Court Ordinances, he was never able to fulfill completely
these early plans. Throughout his tenure of office the specter of economic collapse was uppermost in the thinking of all
British administrators, and Cameron had to give most of his
attention to the problems of declining world prices for peanuts and palm oil products, the two staples on which the economic health of Nigeria depended. He therefore had to modify
his ambitious reform schemes to fit within Nigeria's restricted income.

The first tremors of the worldwide depression had struck
Nigeria by late 1929. During that year the oil traders in
most of the East had suffered a loss in their earnings of
between 8 and 12 percent.[2] At the close of 1930 the price
paid for oil at Calabar had fallen to £12 as contrasted to a
price of over £21 per ton in 1929. A ton of kernels was
worth only £7 compared with over £11 the previous year. Before the market bottomed in the year 1933-34, it was hardly
worth the producer's time to gather and market palm produce.
A ton of first rate oil at Calabar yielded only £3 and kernels dropped to £2 10s per ton in July 1934.[3]

The other staple, peanuts, upon which the Nigerian economy was based was also disastrously affected by world prices
during Sir Donald's tenure. The following table gives some
indication of how depressed the prices were during this
period.[4]

Years	Tons exported	Average price per ton paid at Kano
1930-31	154,000	£4 17s
1931-32	165,000	£6 16s
1932-33	197,000	£5 14s
1933-34	235,000	£2 13s

During the last year of Cameron's administration the price of peanuts improved to the 1931-32 levels, but by then it was too late for the governor to use the added revenue for improvements.

Nigeria's deteriorating financial condition in these years can best be seen by comparing imports and exports for the seven-year period after 1928. These figures are:[5]

Years	Imports (not including Specie)	Exports (not including Specie)
1928	£ 15,765,238	£ 17,075,165
1929	13,219,165	17,756,945
1930	12,616,949	15,028,624
1931	6,510,515	8,771,713
1932	7,194,732	9,476,762
1933	6,339,892	8,727,090
1934	5,363,680	8,873,800

Despite Cameron's plans for reform and the desperate need for change in policy, particularly in the North, he became increasingly tied to the problem of keeping the territory solvent. Nigeria could expect little economic aid from Britain which was facing its own desperate economic crisis. The nature of Britain's position is indicated by the circular letter sent by the Colonial Office to all the colonies requesting those governments to help the mother country in any way possible. Cameron replied that there was no way Nigeria could aid Britain directly. The only valid approach was to try to build up the country in order to increase investment and drastically reduce expenditure. Thus if Nigeria could live within its sharply reduced income it would not be a burden upon the British taxpayers.[6]

Cameron had not been present when the budget for 1931-32 was prepared and approved. Although it called for a restriction of services and of staff at all levels, it did not go far enough. No one could have foreseen in early 1931 how much further prices of raw materials would fall and with them the ability of the government to maintain the level of expenditures of previous years. The result was that, despite new stringencies imposed by Cameron, there was for 1931-32 a huge deficit of £1,330,000. Such a deficit could be absorbed by the accumulated surplus, but it was obvious that deep cuts would have to be made in the operating funds of all departments if Nigeria was not to go bankrupt. So well did Cameron's government gauge the many economic variables that the budget for 1932-33 was balanced, in spite of the slight fall in customs, duties, and railway profits.[7] In addition, taxes were nearly impossible to collect from some northern and most eastern areas because of the inability of the people to accumulate capital. In April 1931, the tax rate in the disaffected areas of the East had been reduced by up to 50 percent. The average standard rate was fixed at four shillings per annum whereas in 1930 it had been generally seven shillings. Even this reduction was not sufficient since in December 1932, 19 percent of the tax due was still outstanding. One year later 44 percent of the tax had not been collected.[8] Cameron in 1934 approved the reduction of the tax rate throughout Owerri Province to only one shilling and sixpence.

Cameron's method of combating the economic ills of Nigeria was in no way innovative. He simply reduced expenditure to meet income. Sir Donald was fortunate in having forty years of experience in administration in which he had come to know the operation of the various departments of government better than did the heads of those departments themselves. This experience proved to be invaluable, and his meticulous work habits and ability to grasp immediately fundamental points certainly aided in planning the various stringencies. Among the small changes he made in late 1932 was the reduction of nine Class II and III officers in the North and five in the South. Cameron also did away with the practice of keeping relief administrators, and as the depression worsened he continued to reduce the size of the administration staff.[9] Another minor adjustment was the abolition of the post of Administrator of the Colony, a position Cameron had once held briefly in 1910. By the early 1930s the office of Administrator was redundant since his minimal duties could easily be done by other central officers.[10] A much more important saving was made by having the central administration retain more of the revenue collected by the northern Native Administrations. Prior to Ormsby-Gore's fact-finding visit in 1926 the Native Administrations had received only 50 percent of the moneys collected. In 1927 their share had been raised to 70 percent. Cameron decided with the approval of the Secretary of State to retain an extra 10 percent from them during the period of the crisis.[11]

In March 1933, a sudden drop in produce prices forced
Cameron to propose the drastic measure of a salary levy.
This levy would affect all personnel and was scaled in the
following manner: first £50--no levy; second £50--4% levy;
next £300--5% levy; next £400--6% levy; next £200--8% levy;
next £500--10% levy; next £1500--12% levy.[12] The Colonial
Office was not enthusiastic about Sir Donald's plan. George
Fiddian, a senior clerk, was particularly perturbed because
Cameron's salary levy was so different from that of the Gold
Coast. In a minute written on 15 April, he wrote that the
Office should demand more explanations from Cameron and concluded with the acid comment, "At any rate, I should not
spare Sir Donald Cameron's feelings or those of the little
knot of Samurai by whom he is surrounded."[13] Fiddian's in-
decision as to whether he should admire Cameron for all his
past achievements or dislike him because he did not immediately bow to the central office bureaucrats is shown in a
further minute of 12 May on the salary levy. He wrote,
". . . if I were not dealing with Sir Donald Cameron I should
say that it [the levy] had all the appearance of being something like panic legislation."[14] Cameron's proposals, despite such protests, were approved and went into effect on
1 June 1933.

If the Colonial Office believed that Cameron was ready
to panic, then it did not fully understand the Nigerian
situation. The state of the economy was becoming worse.
Cameron had expected that with the salary levy and other savings the 1933-34 budget would show a surplus of £15,000. In
September he was informed by his financial advisors that
customs duties would not come up to planned expectations, the
railway deficit would be larger, and collecting taxes in certain parts of Nigeria was impossible. They believed that the
total deficit at the end of the fiscal year would be nearly
£750,000. Such an eventuality would be a disaster since the
total Nigerian surplus was only £2 million. Cameron therefore proposed further drastic budget cuts to the Colonial
Office. These included reductions of 15 percent on Education
and Medical services, and 20 percent on the Nigerian Regiment.
The Secretary of State, Sir Philip Cunliffe-Lister, approved
these new measures, but noted that Cameron had not been send-
ing the Colonial Office monthly financial reports.[15] The
only way one can explain this failure by the Nigerian authorities was that Cameron believed that no monthly report could
possibly indicate the true economic situation of the territory.

In Cunliffe-Lister's communication to Cameron he authorized the governor to use if necessary the Supplementary Sink-
ing Fund of some £900,000 to meet the projected deficit. A

slight upturn in the economy in late 1933, combined with
Cameron's austerity measures, made the situation considerably brighter by the close of the year. It was then projected that the deficit would be a manageable £400,000.[16]
By March 1934, it was obvious that the actual defit would
be approximately £200,000.[17] Cameron's budget for 1934-35
planned for a deficit of slightly over £300,000, well within
the ability of the government to absorb through its accumulated surplus.[18] The year 1934 witnessed the steady rise in
world market prices for Nigeria's two staple crops, peanuts
and palm oil. In February 1934 the price quotation for palm
oil was £12 17s 6d per ton; by January 1935 it had risen to
£20 10s. During the same period, peanut prices rose from
£8 15s to £15 17s 6d per ton.[19] The worst of the depression
was over, and Cameron planned for a balanced budget for the
fiscal year 1935-36. On the eve of his retirement from the
Colonial Service Cameron was congratulated by Cunliffe-Lister
on behalf of the senior staff of the Colonial Office for the
excellent job he had done in maintaining the solvency of
Nigeria.[20]

It is against this background of austerity that one
must evaluate Cameron's modest achievements in social services. Education, which had always been one of his prime
concerns, was especially hard hit by the depression. In
December 1930 there were 191 government and Native Administration schools with a total enrollment of over 15,000 pupils.
By contrast, there were under private ownership 280 schools
which received government assistance, and 2666 schools which
received no state aid, with enrollments of 55,500 and 128,000
students respectively.[21] These figures, it should be noted,
do not include the many Koranic schools in the North. Most
of the schools were elementary schools and were located in
the southern portion of Nigeria. Taking the country as a
whole, only an estimated 9 percent of Nigeria's children were
attending a formal Western type of school. As was the case
in most parts of Africa, the missionaries were responsible
for a large part of the Nigerian educational system. The
bulk of support for their schools came from voluntary contributions from church members in Europe and the United States.
These contributions declined as the depression became worse,
and in 1933 government support also was cut by 15 percent.[22]
Thus many of the smaller mission schools were closed and few
new schools were opened during Cameron's tenure.

There had been a single Education Department for Nigeria
since 1929, but with separate Boards of Education for the
North and South. The northern Board, however, did not meet
until March 1932. The governor's discontent with the administration of the North had some bearing on the decision to
call this first meeting. Cameron was perturbed over the lack
of concern for education evinced by the northern emirs and

105

their British advisors. He was also bothered by the traditional attitudes of almost all groups of Nigerians toward
the education of girls--which was that they should have no
education at all. To coordinate more effectively this phase
of education Cameron's government appointed a lady Superintendent of Schools late in 1931. The governor encouraged
the expansion of elementary teacher training centers at
Ibadan, Uyo, Warri, Katsina, and Bauchi to provide better
training for the staffs of elementary schools. Despite the
financial stringencies, the first groups of students for the
planned Higher College at Yaba were accepted and the contract
let for the first buildings in 1932. Sir Donald officially
opened the college on 19 January 1934, expressing his pleasure at the school and his hopes that it would eventually become a University College.[23]

Medical services for the 20.7 million people of Nigeria
were in an even worse condition than was the educational system. Cities such as Lagos, Abeokuta, Kano, Ibadan, and Enugu
had either government hospitals or dispensaries and various
training programs such as those concerned with infant care.
In the country areas, however, except for the work of medical missionaries, health care was almost nonexistent. In
1929, Dr. Walter Johnson, a specialist in tropical medicine,
visited a number of African territories, both British and
foreign-controlled, to investigate their medical facilities.
He concluded that the northern provinces of Nigeria were
more backward than any. Faced with such desperate health
needs and with concerted opposition to change from traditional leaders, there was little that Cameron could do in
the midst of the depression. Nevertheless, his reorganization of the administration in 1933 and 1934 allowed for the
establishment of Native Authority hospitals. At the end of
1934 there were sixteen such hospitals, out of a total of
twenty-nine, located in the North. Even more important was
the decision to expand the number of Native Authority dispensaries which were funded by local taxes. The choice of
the dispenser generally fell to the Native Authorities; thus
Cameron was able in a modest way to increase low-level medical services while at the same time strengthening the Native
Authorities.[24]

Apart from the ever present specter of the depression,
the most immediate problem confronting Cameron in mid-1931
was how to continue the pacification of those areas in the
East, particularly Owerri and Calabar Provinces, where there
had been the women's disturbances. Using the police, army
units, and special police, Governor Thomson and his successor, Acting Governor Walter Buchanan-Smith, had overawed the
dissatisfied sectors of the East. Army and police units

accompanied by political officers had been given greater
than usual powers by the Peace Preservation Ordinance.
Using these powers and those conferred by the Collective
Punishment Ordinance, the district officers had fined some
villages very heavily for their part in the disturbances.
There was no standard of assessment; each district officer
used his own judgment. Another way the troops impressed the
power of the government on the Ibo and Ibibio was to demolish
or burn the compounds of those suspected of having aided the
women. Thus even before Cameron was appointed governor, the
danger of a general uprising had passed. By mid-1931 the
size of the policing forces in the East had returned to normal strength.[25]

The two Commissions of Inquiry into the causes of the
disturbances, which had been appointed by Governor Thomson,
had completed their work by mid-1930. The longer, more comprehensive report on the background and conduct of affairs
in both Owerri and Calabar Provinces was published in July
1930, and its conclusions were debated by the Legislative
Council in January 1931.[26] Lord Passfield commented extensively on the findings. Although some of his conclusions
were judgments after the fact, it was obvious that he held
Governor Thomson and his staff responsible for instituting
taxation without adequate regard for the feelings of the
people. Passfield noted,

> It appears to me that it was probably injudicious
> and premature to introduce into these Provinces a
> system of direct taxation without at first completing
> a more extensive survey of their social organiza-
> tion.[27]

He went on to note that the views of officers in the field
who were in daily contact with the people had been ignored.
Because it was so difficult to understand the languages and
cultures of the East, the government had devoted less of its
time and energies to the East than it had to less complex
areas in the North and West. The Colonial Secretary in his
official correspondence in 1931 made it very clear that he
wished a complete restudy of the cultures of the Ibo and
Ibibio people and the modes of governing them. He had obviously communicated these feelings and his sense of urgency
to Cameron.

The restudy of the institutions of the eastern areas had
begun in 1930. It was to be conducted in conformance with
the guidelines established in January 1930 by a lengthy memorandum of the Secretary of the Southern Provinces, C. T.
Lawrence.[28] District officers in the East began cautiously

to collect data for the new intelligence reports as soon as the worst of the crises had passed in their areas. Belatedly the central authorities were attempting to understand more of the complex societies of the East. Although Cameron readily concurred in the decision to investigate these cultures, the order to do so did not come from him. District officers in certain of the eastern areas were already far advanced in their researches before Sir Donald arrived in Nigeria in June 1931. What Cameron gave to the investigations was his wholehearted support. He was convinced from the first that Native Administration throughout Nigeria would have to be extensively reorganized and he urged the administrative staff and the few professional anthropologists to provide him with the data on which to base his changes. His enthusiasm and abilities as an administrator had the same effects upon his staff and senior field officers that they had had earlier in Nigeria and Tanganyika. The government staff at all levels knew that their investigations were not window dressing for British politicians, but a very necessary preliminary to reform.

The new spirit of the administration could be seen in Cameron's view of many of the retrogressive or moribund Native Administrations. Even before he had authorized any permanent sweeping changes in the Native Authority and Native Court systems, Cameron had concluded that many of the traditional chiefs would have to be prodded into acting in a more enlightened fashion toward their subjects. The first chance to apply these ideas to a major Native Administration was at Benin. In April 1933, Cameron addressed a long message to the new Oba on the occasion of his installation. This communication, which became known as the Benin Minute, stated in the most delicate terms Cameron's general objectives of administration and explained how Nigerian chiefs should be trained to undertake better the responsibility of government. Cameron announced that he was authorizing the Resident to exercise openly his position as advisor to the Benin Native Administration. The Resident was ordered to take an interest in the day-to-day affairs of the administration, to sit with the Oba in council, and to give advice to the Oba and council.[29] By this pronouncement Cameron established the precedent for Residents all over Nigeria to ease the masquerade of non-involvement in the everyday affairs of government. Henceforth the field staff were charged with direct responsibility in trying to educate the chiefs in Western administrative practice.

Later in 1933, after he had issued his reforming ordinances, Cameron applied the principles of the Benin Minute to Abeokuta and Ijebu-Ode. At Abeokuta, Cameron discussed these proposals with the Alake whom he found to be an intelligent,

progressive ruler. According to Cameron, the Alake welcomed
these ideas of closer harmony between his administration and
that of the British.[30] At Ijebu-Ode there had been turmoil
since the forced removal in 1929 of an Awujale because of
fraud and malpractice. Finally, in early 1933, a new Awujale
was installed who promised to bring the society together
again. Cameron took this opportunity to instruct him in what
the central government expected of him and explain how the
British field staff would operate to help him secure the ends
of good government.[31]

Thus in three of the largest and most important Native
Administrations in western Nigeria Cameron succeeded in making
a profound change without having to alter the basic legislation related to their governance. He merely changed the form
and spirit in which the British agents participated in local
government affairs. In so doing he made clear to his field
staff and the chiefs that much of the change was directed
toward improving government services by educating the chiefs
and their closest advisors. In a similar vein Cameron urged
chiefs and emirs to travel beyond the boundaries of their
small territories. Only by introducing these rulers to the
larger world would they have any basis on which to compare
their own local government and its services. The most dramatic example of Nigerian rulers breaking with their tradition
and visiting other parts of Nigeria was when the Sultan of
Sokoto and the Emir of Gwandu visited Lagos in June 1934.
This was the first time either ruler had made such a long
journey, and neither had ever seen the ocean before.[32]

Sir Donald also traveled as much as possible. This was
but a continuation of a policy he had found so valuable in
Tanganyika. He attended the installations of major chiefs
and spoke at a wide range of ceremonies in every part of
Nigeria. He served a twofold purpose in doing this. First
he could expound his philosophy of government and the reasons
for the changes he was making. But equally important, he
could show himself to people who had never seen a governor
before. He reported on one such journey and its results in
his book:

> Somewhere about 1933 I went down into Owerri Pro-
> vince of Nigeria to have a look at a small Native Admin-
> istration that had recently been formed in the Ibo
> country, meeting the Headmen almost on the spot where
> Dr. Stewart had so brutally been murdered not so many
> months before my arrival in the country in 1908.
> There was an immense crowd. I talked to the Council of
> Elders patiently and simply, and it was very hot and
> dusty and very trying in many other ways. For a long

time I could get no response at all but eventually I
saw a glimmer of interest here and there. At the end
an old gentleman got up and spoke in this sense: 'We
have heard what you said; we are interested. We have
heard that there are governors, that they come and go;
but we have not seen one before. I understand what
you say and I should like to know the name of this
governor.'[33]

After over a quarter of a century of British rule, Cameron
had made a point of showing some of the people of the East
that governors did exist and that they were human and approach-
able.
     The Eleko controversy, which had developed in the years
immediately after World War I, came to the fore again during
the early months of Sir Donald's tenure. The Eleko, traditional ruler of Lagos, had lost almost all political power
in the years following the establishment of the Colony of
Lagos in 1861. The position, however, was an important ceremonial one. Eleko Eshugbayi, perhaps unknowingly, had appeared to be the associate of some of the most radical Western
educated Nigerians in Lagos. This had led to his suspension
from office by Cameron in 1920. Later Sanusi, another des-
cendant of the House of Docemo, had been installed as Eleko.
Nationalists such as Herbert Macaulay, leader of the small
National Democratic Party, and Thomas H. Jackson, editor of
the Lagos Weekly Record, had used the Eleko issue throughout
the 1920s to rally support for their opposition to the un-
representative structure of British government in Nigeria.
Eshugbayi took his case to the courts and after long delays
it reached the Privy Council in March 1931 where it was referred back to the Nigerian Supreme Court for further hearing.
Cameron briefly settled the Eleko problem by a government
announcement on 29 June 1931 to the effect that he was with-
drawing recognition of Sanusi who was Eshugbayi's rival. The
government stipulated that the position of Eleko was being
dispensed with. Eshugbayi and Sanusi would both be considered
merely private citizens and neither could claim to be the
chief representative of the House of Docemo. Sanusi was to
continue to draw his salary, and provision was made to sustain
Eshugbayi on £240 per year. To prevent any legal action by
the parties against the government, the Eshugbayi (Indemnity
for Deportation) Ordinance was passed by the Legislative
Council on 31 July.[34] In October of the following year Eshugbayi died and his supporters asked Sir Donald to support
their new choice, Falolu. Recognizing the ceremonial importance of the position of Eleko and the chance that was presented him to settle the whole question, Cameron appointed

the leading chiefs of Yorubaland to choose a new Eleko. Cameron instructed them that in case of disagreement they should consult the traditional oracle called Ifa. Since only a small proportion of the committee continued to support Sanusi, Cameron accepted the majority recommendation of Falolu. He did this as an "act of grace" stating that Falolu would have "no administrative functions and this recognition has no political significance."[35] With the reception of the new Oba by Sir Donald at Government House in October 1933, the controversy between the government and the people of Lagos concerning the position of the new Eleko finally ended.

Cameron's relations with the northern areas will be detailed later. It is sufficient here to note that he considered the emirates and the paraphernalia of British rule in the North to present him with his most difficult administrative problems. Thus his later revision of the Native Authority and Native Courts Ordinances was directed not at the southern areas, but at the North. He expected and received his most vociferous opposition from British administrators there who could not see the archaic nature of the system and who were afraid that Cameron was tinkering with a finely tuned administrative mechanism. That the Hausa-Fulani administrative structure was tougher than they imagined was illustrated by the affair of the Sultan of Sokoto.

The Sultan, theoretically <u>primus inter pares</u> of the northern rulers, had long been an unsatisfactory ruler. In 1930 it was discovered that he had resorted to various occult practices and was dabbling in magic. Repudiated by his administration, the Sultan fled to the French territory of Niger. He returned to his capital in January 1931 and was accused of using his position to "procure miscarriages of justices [sic]." Reluctantly the British forced the Sultan to abdicate. Again he fled to Niamey but returned to Sokoto later in the year and was removed under a deportation order to Kaduna. The northern Emirs Conference, which had been instituted only in 1930, met at Kaduna in November 1931 and surprised many British administrators by roundly condemning the deeds of their senior colleague, the Sultan, and concurring in the actions of the central authorities. The Emir of Kontagora spoke for most when he stated how deeply he felt the disgrace that the representative of the House of the Shehu dan Fodio had brought upon all the Fulani rulers. The conference recommended that the ex-Sultan be deported from Hausa country.[36] The whole affair illustrated Cameron's basic position that the emirs were in many instances more willing to approve or even institute change than were their British advisors.

111

The most perceptive comment on Cameron's administration in Nigeria was made by Dame Margery Perham soon after her return from her extended study tour of Nigeria in the early 1930s.

> There is, however, a quality in Sir Donald's administration which neither quotation, nor the documents themselves, can wholly convey. It is a compound of realism and humanity which he is able to communicate to the Administration. The circumstances of an African Government are such that it is always in danger of getting a little out of touch with realities, of allowing, as it were, a crust to settle upon the system. The danger is all the greater when the system has been an exceptionally good one. Sir Donald has produced a psychological effect hard to define, in which the crust has been broken and a spirit of self-criticism and of interest in new ideas has been induced. It is a convention of our trusteeship, at least where there is no competing element, that the interest of the natives should be paramount. Sir Donald's work appears to be coloured not by a convention but by a vivid realization of the humanity, individually and in groups, of the people he governs.[37]

Cameron had changed the psychological base of the Nigerian administration as profoundly as he had done earlier in Tanganyika. This alteration allowed him to make the most sweeping changes in the government of Nigeria since Lugard's amalgamation twenty years before.

8

Revision of Nigerian Local Government

Nigeria presented Sir Donald with a wide variety of different but interlocking challenges. Everything was subordinate to the economic crisis, and any hopes that Cameron had of radically altering the method of rule had to wait until the government could bring the financial situation under control. In that interim period, provincial and district officers were kept busy, particularly in the Ibo and Ibibio areas, investigating the bases of traditional rule and law. For almost eighteeen months Cameron made few major changes in the method of governing the protectorate, contenting himself with infusing a new spirit of intelligent planning and bold action in his subordinates. Tied to an almost total concern with finance, he was, nevertheless, planning to introduce sweeping changes at all government levels as soon as it could be done. Cameron's long established working patterns enabled him to absorb tremendous amounts of detail. He read and made pungent marginal notes on almost every Intelligence Report submitted by district authorities.[1] Although Sir Donald accurately saw and reacted to Native Administration in Nigeria as a single problem with variations in different sections of the protectorate, it will be advantageous to view separately his reforms in the South and in the North.

Most of the troops and extra police that had been sent to the East during the crisis had been withdrawn even before Cameron arrived in Nigeria. The Thomson administration had also ordered that investigations be conducted to discover what had caused the disastrous women's uprisings. Cameron encouraged these investigations which were in reality a continuation of the earlier ones that had preceded the general taxation of the East. The important difference after 1930 was in the emphasis of the inquiries. The district staff was more concerned with the people and their political and judicial systems than with imposing a scheme of taxation. Dr. C. K. Meek, the Anthropological Officer for the Northern Provinces, was sent to the East to advise the administration as well as to carry out his own research. He made two thorough investigations himself, one at Nsukka and the other of Owerri Division.[2] However, his greatest service was as an advisor. Most of the reports made by the administrative officers were sent to him before the government would act on the recommendations contained in the reports.

113

By the end of 1933 the central government had received 144 of these "intelligence reports," each of which could be criticized by trained anthropologists. The junior administrators who compiled these reports were not anthropologists. Many of them did not have sufficient command of the African languages to understand the nuances of answers given to them by their respondents. But conditions in most of the eastern areas were such that the reports had to be completed quickly, and however valid the scholarly criticism of the data obtained, it was more than sufficient for Cameron's purposes since his goals were limited and practical. He wanted to learn the mainsprings of organization of the Ibo and Ibibio societies so that the contemplated changes in the Warrant Chief system would be more compatible with their traditional ways of life.

The intelligence reports for 1932 showed that there were no properly established Native Authorities functioning in Owerri Province. For example, Aba, Bende, Owerri, and Ahoada Divisions were divided into Native Court areas, none of which were natural units. In Aba Division this meant that none of the nine Native Courts could demand the natural allegiance of the Ibo villagers in the division. District officers, however, knew the main outlines of the village organizations which were the most important local government agencies for the Ibo and Ibibio. With the active encouragement of the central government the district officers began to encourage village councils to meet and deal with such matters as tax assessments, road upkeep, and plans for future development. Matters affecting an entire division were discussed by meetings of other deliberative groups composed of representatives chosen by village councils in a Native Court area. The Warrant Chiefs who had been so important before the women's disturbances were generally excluded unless they happened by chance to be selected by a village council.[3]

The Resident of Calabar Province in support of his contention that there were no Native Authorities in the generally accepted definition of that term, noted that,

> Throughout the Tribes which inhabit the province the unit is the village, or among the Efiks and Opobos, the "House." Cohesion between groups or villages due to common ancestry or worship, exists and allows the formation of Village Groups and Clans; but nowhere in the Province is there to be found a Group, Clan or Tribal Head whose authority is recognized by the people or one whose power could be used as a focus for local administration.[4]

114

In spite of all difficulties, administrative officers in
Calabar were beginning to use village and clan representatives for communications with the people.

Cameron and the Lagos authorities were thus encouraging
a radical change in the method of administration long before
there was an official change in the Native Authority Ordinance. Government was able to accomplish a great deal in a
short time in establishing these de facto decentralized government units because they had continued to exist during the
long Warrant Chief era. The easy transition in most parts
of the East to the new decentralized form of indirect rule
inaugurated by Cameron was in itself a severe indictment of
the previous British-imposed Warrant Chief system.

Even before Cameron arrived in Nigeria he had been giving serious consideration to the divisive nature of Native
Administration in the North. His first specific concern related to a suggestion originally proposed in 1929 to bring
all non-Africans under the jurisdiction of the northern
Native Courts. This was designed to apply primarily to Asians,
but by extension would also affect Europeans. Sir Graeme
Thomson had asked for Colonial Office advice on the proposal
and Lord Passfield had given approval to the scheme. Thomson,
however, had not had time to reframe the Native Courts Ordinance. Cameron was consulted on this matter before leaving
for Nigeria and vigorously opposed the scheme. In November
1931, Cameron met with Lieutenant-Governor Alexander and his
Residents at Kaduna where the proposal was discussed at
length. In the following month Cameron in a long detailed
dispatch to the new Secretary of State, Sir Philip Cunliffe-
Lister, made clear his unqualified disapproval of the entire
concept.[5] He believed that contrary to Colonial Office opinion, the contemplated change was not minor, but one that
affected "in an important measure the whole future of Nigeria."

Cameron's dispatch of 10 December 1931 is worth looking
at in some detail since in it the governor states some very
general principles. First he opposed having an ordinance
which applied to only one section of Nigeria. Non-Africans
should be treated in the same manner throughout the whole
territory. His major point, however, was that no one seemed
to have considered how the proposal would affect the future
government of Nigeria:

> Up to the present, so far as I am aware, no one
> in authority has seriously directed his mind to a study
> of the absorbing problem of the political evolution of
> Nigeria. Lord Lugard with whom I have discussed the
> matter on more than one occasion since my appointment
> to Nigeria, states quite frankly that the problem was
> not one to which he had to devote his attention when

he was in Nigeria, and that he has not since made any
serious study of it. His successor in the Administration of Nigeria, Sir Hugh Clifford, was not a student
of the principles of Native Administration and in
Malaya had been accustomed to the direct administration
of natives, a sphere in which he achieved eminent success and a distinguished reputation. My immediate predecessor was not absorbed in the study of the principles
of Native Administration.[6]

Sir Donald went on in that dispatch to point out that
no one could foretell the future with exactitude. He did
not know whether the government would evolve in the direction
of Western institutions or whether there would be step by
step developments toward a "Native Council for the whole Protectorate." He believed that the government should nevertheless avoid adopting measures which they knew would have divisive effects. He added a devastating comment on Thomson's
administration when he wrote, "Pretence has been a feature
of the administration in Nigeria during the last few years--
as I have already pointed out in previous despatches--and is
a dangerous thing."[7] This heretical honesty so shocked a
Colonial Office official that he noted in the margins of the
dispatch, "Really this is too strong." Another official
minuted, "He [Cameron] is too fond of running down his predecessors (and successors!) and asking one to believe that
he and he alone, can do anything!"[8] This was a somewhat
emotional comment, since Cameron was merely pointing out obvious shortcomings of the Nigerian administration and stating an. expert opinion on what he considered poor legislation.
Despite the attitude of some persons in the Colonial Office
toward Sir Donald, the suggestion to bring Asians and Europeans under the jurisdiction of the emirs' courts was not
seriously considered again.

By the beginning of 1933 Cameron had a mass of information which strongly indicted the previous centralized government of the East. He also had a large number of intelligence
reports and correspondence from his field staff which indicated that the de facto system was working. By collating
this information with the data he had obtained from intelligence reports submitted by district officers on the details
of local government in the North, Cameron established a sound
basis for the series of ordinances which in 1933 officially
gave the entire protectorate system a new methodology and a
new series of goals.

From the first days of his administration Cameron decided to use the Legislative Council more directly than had
his predecessors. He was still suspicious of many of the
Western educated Nigerians and their role in the future

government of Nigeria. However, he did not ignore them nor
did he wish to restrict the activities of the Legislative
Council. After one session on administration, one of the
African unofficial members stated, "I knew little of this
thing before that was of any value to me. I disliked it
because I was imperfectly informed. I understand the policy
after reading this memorandum and I gladly accord my support
to it."[9] Cameron later related that one result of this
better rapport with the Africans on the Legislative Council
was a series of investigations into applying indirect rule
to portions of the Colony. Similar proposals had been rejected ten years before, but owing to Cameron's policy of
informing the members in detail of the basis of proposed
legislation, the council after Cameron had left Nigeria
approved his proposals for indirect administration for parts
of the Colony.

One of the most revealing evidences of the governor's
hopes and plans for northern Nigeria occurred in a speech to
the Legislative Council on 6 March 1933 setting out his reforms of the Native Administration. Cameron was very candid
with the council, particularly with reference to Native Administration in the North. Sir Donald remarked that

. . . in some measure we have departed from the intentions and principles of Lord Lugard in this
respect; particularly into drifting into the habit
of mind--and I use the word "drift" with intent--
into drifting into the habit of mind that a "feudal
monarchy" of this kind [the northern emirates] . . .
is the be-all and end-all of Indirect Administration.[10]

Cameron continued by castigating the British officials in
the North for their general attitudes. He stated that the
policy accepted by many administrators that the

Moslem Administrations should be sheltered as
far as possible from contact with the outside world
--the century-old doctrine of political untouch-
ability--was due, no doubt to a feeling, however un-
formulated, that an unreformed "feudal monarchy"
could not expect to stand up against the natural
forces of a Western civilization that was gradually
but quite preceptibly creeping further north in
Nigeria.[11]

Cameron informed the Legislative Council of his unrestricted
opposition to such ideas. The government must provide the

117

necessary machinery through which constructive change could
be accomplished. More than anything else, British officials
should try to provide the appropriate support and guidance
for that change through the Native Administrations. He noted
that Residents could do only so much in a limited time to
impress Native Authorities with the need for change and that
one of the primary duties of a Native Authority was the
"amelioration of social and economic conditions" of the
people. Impetus for reform, however, "must come from within,
from the Native Administration itself."[12]

The Nigerian Daily Times, reporting rather floridly the
governor's proposals for altering the system of indirect
rule, referred to his speech as "the great charter of liberty
for the native people in this country" and compared the contemplated changes to those accomplished by Edwin Montagu
and Lord Chelmsford in India.[13] Cameron would have dis-
claimed any such exaggeration both in regard to his intent
and also the probable effects of his legislation. The article
is, however, important in that it shows the popularity of
the proposed reforms with a large segment of educated Lago-
sians. The article concluded with the laudatory comment,

> So big a step in colonial administrative admin-
> istration could only have been conceived and carried
> out by a big, just and courageous mind and by a man
> who not only has a genuine sympathy with the progress
> of the African people but has a strong faith in their
> ability to make full use of the advantages and oppor-
> tunities offered to them.[14]

Even prior to his significant speech before the Legislative Council Cameron had moved to alter the structure of
Nigerian administration. He believed that the title Lieutenant-Governor conveyed too much to the holders as well as to
the Nigerian population. He proposed that this title be
abolished whenever the incumbents of those offices should
retire. The new title would be the less prestigious one of
Chief Commissioner since lieutenant-governors held their commission from the Crown whereas a chief commissioner would
hold his from the Colonial Secretary. The Secretary of State
approved this proposal in June 1933.[15] Since Alexander had
already retired, Cameron immediately appointed George Browne
to be the Chief Commissioner in the North. Walter Buchanan-
Smith remained as Lieutenant-Governor of the Southern Provinces until his retirement in 1935. This difference in
titles made it easier for Cameron to upgrade Buchanan-Smith's
position. In the governor's absence, he would rank directly
behind the Chief Secretary, but ahead of the Chief Commissioner of the Northern Provinces.

In a sense 1933 was Cameron's "year of miracles" in Nigeria. Not since the formation of the protectorates had there been so many fundamental changes in the mechanisms of rule. Although there was subsidiary legislation, six major ordinances which dealt with Native Administration and Courts defined Sir Donald's basic concepts of government. The least important of these was Ordinance No. 26 of 1933 which enabled the governor to appoint any administrative officer to exercise full powers of a Native Authority where there was no such authority.[16] Such a measure, which Cameron considered transitory, was necessary for the government of some parts of the East and some of the northern "pagan" areas.

The key ordinance for revising the administration of the protectorate areas was the Native Authority Ordinance No. 43 of 1933.[17] It repealed the old general ordinance and reenacted most of its provisions in a new form. The new ordinance was considerably more flexible than its predecessor and facilitated the establishment of widely divergent types of local government in different parts of Nigeria. It specifically underwrote the major alterations already underway in the East. By the close of 1934 the reorganization of those areas presented a totally different governing structure than two years before. Throughout the East, wherever possible, administrative and court divisions were based on clan divisions and below this, on an even lower level, the village. One can appreciate the complexity of the new eastern local government organization by observing Aba Division alone where there were five distinct clans and dozens of villages. By the time the reorganization of Owerri Province was completed there were 245 Native Authorities and sub-authorities.[18]

Such Native Authorities as the Calabar Council with 167 members would have been anathema to British administrators during Graeme Thomson's administration.[19] They would have considered such a large body to be too unwieldy to be functional. This, however, was not the case. The Ibo and Ibibio people had been accustomed to such large representative bodies. The size of the councils guaranteed that no one man, such as Native Court clerk, could dominate the Authority and force his opinion on a small group of poorly educated nonrepresentative members. Decisions taken by such Native Authorities were acceptable to the people since they had been arrived at by their own leaders and not by the fiat of a few arbitrarily appointed Warrant Chiefs whose authority derived from the support of the district officer.

In the more highly structured governments of the West and North the Native Authority Ordinance did not result in major organizational changes. What it did was to make the Residents clearly agents of the central government. Ordinance

119

No. 43, in conjunction with the new legislation related to
the Courts, attempted to curb the Residents' powers as judges
and indirect rulers. It also very clearly halted the development of separate emirates into sovereign states. The emirates
in theory became just one particular example of local government, and the Residents were charged to foster, wherever possible, development from below for the benefit of the people
and not just the chiefs.[20]

Cameron insisted that the "sealed pattern" emirate was
not the best or only form of administration for the North and
demanded that his Residents and district officers in pagan
areas should search for the rudiments of traditional rule.
Once such elements of traditional government and society of
the hill and pagan tribes had been discovered they were to
be encouraged. He also insisted that the emirs relinquish
an adequate degree of autonomy in local affairs to the clan
and tribal councils so that they could function properly.
Sir Bryan Sharwood-Smith, later Governor of the Northern
Region and no great supporter of Cameron, considered the new
spirit of self-questioning forced on the northern administration to be Cameron's greatest achievement. He believed this
to be most true of the administration of the "pagan" regions.[21]

Correlate with the reform of Native Authorities was an
even more fundamental reorganization of the courts system of
Nigeria. This was achieved by four ordinances of which the
most important for most Nigerians was the Native Courts Ordinance No. 44 of 1933.[22] It established four grades of courts.
Class A courts had full judicial powers in all civil actions
and criminal cases including the death penalty. Class B
courts had complete jurisdiction only in inheritance, estate
management, traditional marriage, and civil claims where no
money was involved. Full jurisdiction over these matters
was also given to class C and D courts. Otherwise class B
courts were restricted to deal only with civil cases where
demand or damages did not exceed £100. In criminal cases
class B courts had jurisdiction only where the punishment did
not exceed twelve strokes or a fine of £50 or imprisonment
for not more than one year. Class C courts, although possessing full powers when dealing with a variety of minor cases,
could handle most civil cases only if the damage was less
than £50 and criminal cases where the punishment was not more
than six months imprisonment. Class D courts had even more
limited jurisdiction, generally having powers only over civil
cases where the fine did not exceed £25 and criminal cases
where a sentence of imprisonment would not be over three
months duration.

The ordinance did not explicitly restrict A and B class
courts to any part of the territory. However there were no
A class courts operating in the East during Cameron's tenure.

There clan courts were designated C grade and the village courts were D grade. The most important of the class A courts were located in the North where the chief Alkali of each emirate presided. In most northern districts there were also Alkali courts which had grade B powers. All records, complaints and appeals were forwarded from these courts to the Waziri's office located in the chief city of the emirate. The Waziri in consultation with the emir then decided on what further action should be taken on individual cases.[23]

Cameron had for some time been critical of the appelate system in Nigeria. Too many Africans were at the mercy of decisions rendered by the court of first instance. Again the North, with its seventeen courts with full powers and no appeal from their decisions, in his opinion was the greatest offender. Of this he wrote,

> In those areas the jurisdiction of this High Court is ruled out so far as Africans are concerned. It is not in the interest of the Emirates concerned that an inferior system of justice should prevail in them as compared with the rest of Nigeria, that is, that in those particular areas alone an African may not have the same rights of appeal to a higher court as he has elsewhere in Nigeria . . . An African should not merely because he is living in a first class emirate possess rights which are inferior to those that his fellows enjoy outside it.[24]

Ordinance Nos. 45, 46, and 47 of 1933 spelled out in great detail the further reform of the Nigerian courts system. They were particularly concerned with the appelate process. Ordinance No. 45, the Protectorate Courts Ordinance, abolished as of 31 March 1934 the old Provincial Courts.[25] It created a number of lesser courts of first instance called Magistrates Courts and also the High Court of the Protectorate, the most important court of the protectorate. These courts were designed to exercise special functions in the towns and to handle all major cases that could not be served by the Native Courts. Ordinance No. 45 curtailed the powers of administrative officers to act in a judicial capacity except in very remote areas. Major power was given to the judges and assistant judges of the Magistrate and High Courts. The new Protectorate Courts became closely linked with the various Native Courts since the right of appeal of litigants from the decisions of the lower courts to the High Court was guaranteed. Legal practitioners were barred from appearing in any of the Native Courts, no matter their class. They were, however, allowed to appear for clients in the Magistrates and High Courts. Ordinance No. 46 ended the powers of the Supreme Court in the protectorate except in certain specified cases.[26] It became the major court of the Colony area. Ordinance No. 47 provided for appeal from certain decisions of the Protectorate High Court or the Supreme Court to the West African Court of Appeal.[27]

By means of these ordinances, Cameron and his associates created a completely integrated court system for Nigeria. It allowed for maximum diversity from the levels of the village, clan, or emirate, where African leaders gave decisions according to traditional or Islamic law, to appeals to various levels including the West African Appellate Court. In devising the new Nigerian courts Cameron departed from the philosophy he had followed in reorganizing the Tanganyika court system. There he had given maximum authority to the Residents and district officers and had attempted, as far as possible, to keep professional magistrates from acting directly in an appellate capacity. This difference in approach perturbed Cameron's critics and even some of his friends. The reason for the different approach lies in the truism that Nigeria was not Tanganyika and the fact that Cameron viewed indirect rule as a pragmatic, flexible concept designed to meet specific institutional problems. In Tanganyika Cameron was building an administrative and judicial structure on only very rudimentary systems provided by the Arabs, Germans, and his immediate predecessor. Faced with the multiplicity of differing cultures, he decided that the administrative field staff knew more of the people with whom they served than did magistrates at Dar es Salaam, Tabora, or Arusha. In Nigeria he had to revise a long established system without upsetting to too great a degree the great emirates or Yoruba chiefdoms while at the same time providing the flexibility necessary for the eastern areas.

The governor obviously had other reasons for attempting to divorce his administrative staff from the judicial system. As already noted, Cameron believed the North was becoming a series of small feudal states within the state. He wanted to check this tendency and knew that many of the older professional field officers in the North disagreed with his policy. He felt that they should be divorced as far as possible from influencing African rulers. In the speech before the Legislative Council on 6 March 1933 he gave his opinion of politically biased persons influencing court decisions:

> If the decision of the Court may properly be swayed by political or other non-juridical consideration within the knowledge of the administrative officer . . . then, in my judgment, the court has ceased to be a judicial tribunal and the officer has ceased to be a judicial officer.[28]

Sir Donald did not wish officers in the North to continue to blur what he considered the necessary distinctions
between Native Administration and the overlapping but distinct
system of justice. He later wrote,

> I personally care nothing whether the presiding
> officer of the Court is called administrative officer,
> magistrate (as in East Africa and now in Nigeria), or
> judge, so long as he is an officer who has shown compe-
> tence in weighing evidence, and so long as he arrives at
> his decision in accordance with the weight of evidence
> he has recorded, and not for reasons which are not on
> the record. It is obvious that if his decision is not
> based on the recorded evidence it must be upset unless
> the inferior courts are withdrawn from the supervision
> of the High Court judges; unless, in short, the African
> is deprived of the protection of a court administering
> justice in accordance with judicial standards, and again
> placed at the mercy of the executive.[29]

This attitude, combined with the necessity to find suitable
magistrates for the greatly expanded Protectorate Courts system, led to a type of apprenticeship system. Those members
of the civil service who wished to and who had previous law
training could be appointed to act as a judge in a Magistrate
Court. Some, after showing their talents, would become
assistant judges of the High Court of the Protectorate.
Finally, if they had proved qualified they could become full
judges of that court.[30]

Redistricting was undertaken at the same time as the
administrative and judicial reforms. Some measures had already been taken prior to 1931 in the eastern areas where
new Native Courts had been created to represent more accurately homogenous clans. Most redistricting in the East was
on the Native Court level although there were some transfers
of clans from one province to another. Thus in 1933 the
towns of Mbula and Achara of the Isualtu clan and the entire
Umuchieze clan were shifted from Awgu Division of Onitsha
Province to Owerri Province.[31] Although it could not completely eradicate previous errors, redistricting of the East
did provide administrative units reasonably reflective of
clan organization. These alterations, combined with the
radical changes in the composition of the Native Courts and
the restructuring of Native Authorities, allowed the Ibo,
Ijaw, and Ibibio more freedom on the local government level
than at any time since they had been under British protection.

Redrawing boundaries and creating new forms of local
administration was even more complex in northern Nigeria.

In 1933 a new division was formed in Benue Province composed of Lafia Emirate and the independent districts of Awe. The Emirates of Yauri and Dabai were transferred from the defunct Sokoto Southern Division to Gwandu and Sokoto Division. At the same time the towns of Makurdi and Abinsi were given separate administration by councils under the presidency of chiefs.[32] Kano Province was reorganized by shifting one emirate in the northern areas to Kano Division, while in Zaria Province the district boundaries were readjusted to unite as far as possible people with close ethnic affinities. A new Province of Katsina was created by separating it from Zaria Province.[33] In the Tiv and Plateau areas there was considerable reorganization in 1934 and 1935. A new Tiv Division was created on 1 April 1934 composed of the old Abinisi Division associated with independent Tiv districts. This reform brought most of the Tiv people together in one division, and, combined with the redesign of Tiv Native Administration to include clan and village councils in the thirty-four districts, gave the Tiv relative freedom from domination by the Hausa-Fulani.[34] At the same time in the Plateau Province eleven independent Bironi speaking districts were fused into the Bironi tribal area with seventeen tribal courts. In the same province, the Sura District was divided into two separate and independent unions of people. The Hill Angas and Kaleri tribes of the Plateau Province were also completely reorganized. In Shendon Division there was also a federation of the closely related "pagan" Namu and Dummuk tribes.[35] During the last two years of Cameron's administration such changes in boundaries and methodology profoundly altered the entire nature of British rule in the North. It was not surprising that many of the northern senior administrative officers resented Cameron and considered him to be a blundering iconoclast who had no reverence for northern tradition or for Lord Lugard, the creator of the system of indirect rule.

There are indications at this time of a growing coolness in the relations between Sir Donald and Lord Lugard. There had for some time been confusion over which of the two men was actually responsible for certain types of administrative practices. Lugard tended to get official credit for the institution of policies over which he had no control and with which he might have disagreed. But Lugard had a national reputation whereas Cameron was known by a relatively few persons. Dame Margery Perham remembers how surprised she was by receiving a sharp letter of reprimand from Cameron over an article she had written praising him for his work in Tanganyika. She had remarked how well he had carried out Lord Lugard's ideas. Sir Donald informed her that what he had

124

done in Tanganyika was in accordance with his own ideas and he did not owe the impetus for reform to anyone else.[36] This probably was not just a testy letter, but the reaction of a proud man who felt he was being reduced to the level of a practitioner rather than a creator. Much later Governor Sir Arthur Richards, in making proposals for a new Constitution for Nigeria, made specific reference to Lugard and the debt he owed to Lugard's ideas.[37] If Cameron was aware of this comment in 1944 he probably, after the anger subsided, received cynical pleasure from the fact that his successors Bourdillon and Richards were operating a system which he, Cameron, had devised--one that Lugard did not like.

In a confidential letter in September 1933 to Sir Cyril Bottomley, a senior official in the Colonial Office, Cameron asked permission to reissue his Political Memorandum on the Principles of Native Administration in an updated form. He had originally issued it soon after his arrival in 1931 and he wanted the revised work to be available for the field staff even though the revision would not be ready until just before his tour of duty ended. The Colonial Office gave their reluctant approval, and this in itself was a small triumph for continuity of policy. Cameron's letter contained some stinging references to Lugard's earlier Memorandum on Native Administration and how much mischief it had done by being applied to the southern areas since it had been designed primarily for the Muslim North. The last paragraph of this letter stated,

> I do not know if the Colonial Office ever consults Lugard in these days. If so, I should warn you that he appears to dislike my Address to the Legislative Council and detests my judicial reforms.[38]

Cameron added the last sentence by hand which said, "In fact he has dropped me as a correspondent." One can appreciate the wonderment of Sir Cyril Bottomley and others at the Colonial Office at this turn of affairs since they were hard pressed to find any substantial differences between the philosophies of Cameron and Lugard.

During the last year of his administration a situation developed which caused Cameron and the Colonial Office acute embarrassment and which detracted from Sir Donald's personal reputation and, he believed, threatened an appreciation of his genuine accomplishments. Two English businessmen charged that Cameron had slandered them and brought action against him in the courts. The case, details of which fill two large files of documents, was simple, but its resolution was complex.[39]

125

The entrepreneurs, Cyril Bowley and William Riegels, had been associated with a firm, Onitsha Industries, which in 1934 had gone bankrupt and was in the process of liquidation. Bowley and Riegels were charged with fraud. They were later convicted of this, but the decision was reversed by a higher court. Before the affair of Onitsha Industries had been re-solved, Bowley visited the governor with another scheme. He and Riegels planned to form a new company to grow and export maize, and they wanted government approval. There is no record of the exact conversation, but Cameron's comments must have been quite direct. He was convinced that Onitsha Indus-tries had previously defrauded hundreds of Africans, and now one of the men most responsible had the temerity to approach him for his approval of another questionable venture. An educated estimate of Cameron's statements to Bowley would be that they left no doubt of the governor's contempt for the man.

Bowley and Riegels soon afterward filed suit against Cameron claiming that he had damaged their reputations. While on leave in the late spring of 1934 Cameron discussed the pending litigation in detail with the Colonial Office. He was assured of the finest counsel and that all costs would be borne by the government. Throughout the remainder of the year the legal staffs for both Cameron and his accusers were extremely busy preparing their cases. With so much time and effort devoted to ostensibly a very small matter, the outcome was definitely anti-climatic. The action against Cameron was dismissed because of the failure of the plaintiffs to enter the necessary letters of request in the time granted them. The entire costs of the proceedings fell on Bowley and Riegels, but since they were bankrupt the government assumed the expense of the ill-conceived action. Throughout the embarrassing affair Cameron maintained a cool aloofness, convinced that he had done nothing wrong and had only dealt justly with a pair of businessmen whose past record of deal-ings with Africans justified nothing but his contempt. It is obvious by his insistence upon having the dismissal action published that he was fully aware of the damaging nature of the charges and that in the minds of persons who disliked him and suspected his motives he could never be entirely vindi-cated. Cameron sincerely believed that the litigation had damaged his credibility with his superiors.

In a more important area Cameron could feel thwarted since he knew he had not finished the foundations for the complete reform of Nigeria's administration. One problem he never investigated thoroughly was how the central government machinery in native areas could interact most efficiently with local government functions. He was aware of the bad effects upon government of creating a situation where the Residents' powers were completely derived from the central authority. I. F. Nicolson has speculated that Cameron's further government reorganization perhaps would have been along the lines of Governor Egerton's system of strengthening the provinces by allowing each to develop into an effective unit of government. Cameron was always openly respectful of Egerton and indicated in his book deep admiration of the early system of provincial commissioners.[40] Sir Donald did not have the time, however, to tackle this delicate problem before the expiration of his term of office. When Cameron left Nigeria in 1935 his task of remodeling the administrative structure of Nigeria was thus incomplete. His successor, Sir Bernard Bourdillon, made only one major change in the administrative system he inherited from Cameron. This was the division in 1939 of southern Nigeria into two parts with the Niger River as the boundary between East and West. However deeply Cameron felt about leaving Nigeria with part of his task undone, he could take comfort in the fact that his Native Authority and Courts Ordinances of 1933 gave Nigeria the most totally integrated, rational administrative system it was to have during the long period of British rule.

One should not believe that in the short space of four years Cameron was able to convince the more conservative British administrators and African rulers to accept completely his new programs. Sir Bryan Sharwood-Smith noted that many of Cameron's reforms in the North "had less significance in practice than on paper."[41] The district officers in their own areas remained the key fact of British administration and they tended inevitably to be greatly influenced by the people they helped govern. Neither Governor Richards nor Governor Bourdillon was as passionately devoted to improving the Native Authority system as Cameron had been. Thus in many cases the field staff paid only lip service to the spirit of Cameron's reforms, and those powerful African rulers who wished little or no change in the way they ruled their areas were supported by the British field staff in their territory. The most dramatic change wrought by Cameron's reforms occurred in the East after 1935. Given a semblance of their old political system and the opportunity for individuals to get ahead, a growing number of Ibo and Ibibio young and old accepted partial Westernization as the key to the future. The West was more hesitant and the North the most reluctant to accept Cameron's dictum that the only way for the traditional authorities to remain viable was to change to meet new challenges. It is hard to escape the conclusion that when Cameron departed from Nigeria much of the drive and spirit for modernization of the Native Authorities went with him. Apathy combined with the stringencies of World War II made the Native Authority system the anachronism noted by Western educated African nationalists in the immediate post war period. British support for the traditional leaders at the expense of the Western educated minority lasted for only a decade and a half after Cameron left Nigeria. He was one of the last British administrators who truly believed that African traditional government could become the basis for national as well as local rule.

Epilogue

Sir Donald and Lady Cameron left Nigeria in 1935 for a retirement that had been postponed by his four arduous years as governor. Cameron had been nearly exhausted at the end of his tour in Tanganyika, but there is no indication that he was in ill health or particularly depressed at the thought of retirement after forty-three years of service. At the end of any long active career there are bound to be regrets, as well as serious questioning of what to do with the time now that the discipline of work is no longer present. Cameron for his part must have believed that the Colonial Office would take advantage of his long experience and obvious success in governing two of the most difficult African territories. He could look to Lugard as an example of a man who was as active and productive after retirement as before.

After the accolades for his excellent work in Nigeria had died away, the Colonial Office tended to ignore Cameron. He was appointed to the Education Advisory Committee and became Vice-Chairman of the Governing Body of the Imperial College of Agriculture. However important these posts might have been, they could not occupy the full attention of a man who had developed such compulsive work habits as had Sir Donald. In the three years after leaving Nigeria, some of Cameron's time was devoted to writing and preparing the manuscript of My Tanganyika Service and Some Nigeria. He was also occasionally called upon to be a speaker or a member of a panel at conferences concerned with governing the empire.

It is not possible to know definitely why the Colonial Office did not make more use of Cameron's talents in the decade after his retirement. Many former governors with less ability than Cameron were used more by the service. The first inclination is to blame the Colonial Office for not taking proper advantage of the talent available to it, but it is likely that other factors were involved. In 1935 the Conservative Party succeeded a coalition of Conservatives and Labour which had been formed in the face of the economic crisis. Cameron had always received his staunchest support from the Labor Party and most opposition from the Conservatives. It is also undoubtedly true that Sir Donald had, in the course of his administrations, made enemies who later became very influential and who would not necessarily wish him well. We do not know of Cameron's attitude toward accepting invitations from the government to act as a consultant in the period immeidately after his retirement. If he adopted the posture of wanting to be left alone, then there is little wonder that his services were not asked for later on. There is also the fact of Cameron's personality. He had been used to having his own way. Many people considered him overbearing since he did not attempt to conceal his dislike for those he considered foolish. He was in reality a retiring personality who adopted the facade of harshness, but a new generation of officials can hardly be blamed for not wanting to suffer from his sharp tongue and mordant wit.

In retrospect it is a minor tragedy that Cameron's talents were, for whatever reason, not used more fully either by government or private industry. Most governors had well-developed interests aside from their work. They hunted, fished, traveled, farmed, wrote, or collected things. Cameron had never developed a fondness for anything unconnected with his work. Those who served with Cameron do not remember, apart from his liking billiards, that he ever had any particular outside interest. G. S. Sayers noted that had Sir Donald the inclination, he would have made his mark as a company director.[1] Yet he does not seem ever to have explored the possibility of going into business. Cameron's failing eyesight in the ten years before his death greatly restricted his ability to undertake new tasks. The closing years of his life were anti-climatic and non-productive.

Sir Donald's only son, Geoffrey Valentine, a shadowy figure remembered by only a few of Cameron's associates, had entered the law. In the early part of World War II he had become the legal secretary to the government of Malta. In May 1941, his plane disappeared at sea, presumably destroyed by German or Italian aircraft. Sir Donald obviously accepted this grievous event with the stoicism so common to him, but the news appears to have completely undermined Lady Cameron who was almost immediately hospitalized and remained under organized medical care for the rest of her life.

Cameron's special kind of humor as well as his loneliness during the latter years of his life are remembered by some acquaintances. Dr. Anthony Sillery recalls that he was always glad to talk to men who had served under him. At his club, the East India and Sports Club, he tended to play games with his blindness. He knew, for example, exactly when enough water had been added to his gin.[2] Cameron, who had always been against pretense, carried with him in his old age his many prejudices against individuals with whom he had served. One habit which obviously gave him much delight, although it embarrassed his friends, was to talk to them at length and in a very loud voice about the shortcomings of some of the people he disliked. Many of those who were the objects of Cameron's verbal scorn were also members of the same club.[3]

Cameron's humor as well as his sense of responsibility was reflected in his will executed in November 1945 and the codicil to it dated February 1947.[4] The bulk of his estate was to be used to maintain Lady Cameron under "continuous medical care." He bequeathed to his two sisters and nephews and grandnieces small sums which were to be increased only slightly after his wife's death. After Lady Cameron no longer needed it, the bulk of the estate was to go to organizations Cameron admired. The sum of £3000 was to be held in trust for Makerere College if it received a Royal Charter. If not, the sum was to revert to the Tanganyika government for the furtherance of African education. An additional £1000 duty free was given to the R.A.F. benevolent fund "as a tribute to the skill and valour of the so few." The residue of his estate was bequeathed to the Church Missionary Society for missionary work in southern Nigeria.

The codicil of 1947 changed only two major items of the original will. The Church Missionary Society was left only £1000 to be devoted specifically to medical work. Obviously the Society's plans for Nigeria had irked him since he noted as reason for the change that "I do not approve of grandiose building." The second alteration in the will concerned the disposal of his body. Originally he had intended for it to be cremated. The codicil specified that it be handed over to Charing Cross Hospital for scientific research. Sir Donald Charles Cameron, G.C.M.G., aged seventy-five, died on 8 January 1948, and the wishes expressed in the codicil of the previous year were carried out.

Cameron's active political life had ended thirteen years before his death. In that period the man might have been considered an anachronism by some; even the work he had done was beginning to be called into question by African nationalism and a new spirit of accommodation on the part of the British government. It is worth noting, however, that even the most severe critics of indirect rule have tended to spare Cameron. No less a person than Julius Nyerere, certainly no friend of the British imperial system, has stated that Cameron was one of two governors who made genuine contributions to Tanzania.[5] Underlying most of the comments on Cameron made by opponents as well as friends was the recognition of his intelligence, honesty, and dedication. Perhaps it is well to close this brief study of Sir Donald Cameron not with a sympathetic judgment by the author, but with expressions of appreciation of these qualities by persons who either worked with him or knew him well.

Lord Altrincham (Sir Edward Grigg), ex-Governor of Kenya, writing in Kenya's Opportunity, remarked,

131

It remains to assess the achievement of a visionary as intrepid as any Don Quixote, since Cameron was exactly that. My own judgement [sic] is that he was right in all respects but one [closer union] and that his achievement will stand for all time as a monument to British leadership in Africa, provided we ourselves do not destroy it from addiction to that fetish of Parliamentary government which he so bitterly denounced.[6]

Sir Philip Mitchell, who governed Fiji, Kenya, and Uganda, explaining why Cameron's ideas were not carried out as he visualized them, stated,

We cannot have a world war every twenty-five years and hope for long term Colonial policies to have in all respects the results for which we devised them; and as the Swahili proverb says, 'When the elephants fight the grass is trampled.'. . . There have lived great men after (if I may paraphras_) Agamemnon, but the legacy Cameron bequeathed to the country [Tanganyika] was one that has proved of incalculable value to it.[7]

Dr. Anthony Sillery, former Administrative Officer in Tanganyika and subsequently Resident Commissioner in Bechaunaland and Sir John Nicoll, Administrative Officer in Tanganyika and ex-Governor of Singapore, in a letter to The Times, 1961, wrote,

In the chorus of mutual congratulation that will greet the arrangements for independence in Tanganyika, it is hoped that the name of Sir Donald Cameron, who was Governor from 1925 to 1931, will not be forgotten. Many who served under him and revere his memory regard his passionate yet informed devotion to African interests, his insistence on the preparation of Africans for high responsibilities, and his resistance to racial discrimination as the chief factors in creating the atmosphere in which his successors have been able to effect a smooth transition to self-government and eventual independence.[8]

Gerald F. Sayers, former Administrative Officer in Tanganyika, editor of The Tanganyika Handbook, and former Commonwealth Affairs Advisor to the Conservative Party, commented,

Cameron knew his own mind, and pursued his aims wholeheartedly. He would have made a name for himself, I think in any walk of life, and there are few Colonial governors in the 25 years in which I was a member of the Service who could hold a candle to him.[9]

Sir Donald's career undoubtedly showed to the best advantage the highest ideals of service, sacrifice, and concern, which the Colonial Service asked of its senior officers but seldom received. His administrations in Africa were models of logic and clarity operated within the context of an overall system that was not always distinguished by these qualities. Most important, he was an interesting, intelligent person whose rough exterior could not hide the humanity which was the driving force behind his actions. Nigeria and Tanganyika were well served by such a man.

LAKE
CHAD

Sokoto   Katsina

S O K O T O   K A N O   B O R N U

Kano   Maiduguri

Zaria
Z A R I A

N I G E R   Kaduna   B A U C H I   Bauchi

I L O R I N   Niger R   PLATEAU   Benue R   Yola

CAMEROON
MANDATE

Ilorin   ADAMAWA

Oyo
O Y O   Ife   KABBA   B E N U E

ABEO-   Ibadan   ONDO
KUTA   BENIN   ONIT-
SHA   CAMEROON MANDATE

Lagos   Benin   Ogoja
LAGOS   Enugu   OGOJA
COLONY   Onitsha

IJEBU-ODE   WARRI
OWERRI   CALABAR

Calabar
GULF   NIGERIAN
OF   PROVINCES
GUINEA   Brass

0   100
MILES

Appendix 1
KEY COLONIAL ADMINISTRATORS, 1912-1939

YEAR	BRITISH PARTY IN POWER	PRIME MINISTER	SEC. OF STATE FOR COLONIES	PERMANENT UNDERSECRETARY	GOVERNOR OF NIGERIA	GOVERNOR OF TANGANYIKA	GOVERNOR OF KENYA	GOVERNOR OF UGANDA
1912	LIBERAL	H.H. ASQUITH	LORD HARCOURT	J. ANDERSON	LORD LUGARD	GERMAN RULE	HENRY BELFIELD	FREDERICK JACKSON
13								
14						MILITARY GOVERNMENT		
15			A. BONAR LAW					
16								
17	NATIONAL COALITION	DAVID LLOYD GEORGE	WALTER LONG	GEORGE FIDDES		HORACE BYATT	CHARLES BOWRING	ROBERT CORYNDON
18								
19	LLOYD GEORGE LIBERALS & CONSERVATIVE		LORD MILNER		HUGH CLIFFORD		EDWARD NORTHEY	
1920								
21			W. CHURCHILL	JOHN MASTERSON-SMITH				GEOFFREY ARCHER
22	CONSERVATIVE	A. BONAR LAW	DUKE OF DEVONSHIRE					
23		S. BALDWIN						
24	LABOUR	R. MACDONALD	J. H. THOMAS	SAMUEL WILSON		DONALD CAMERON		
25	CONSERVATIVE	STANLEY BALDWIN	LEOPOLD AMERY		GRAEME THOMSON		EDWARD GRIGG	WILLIAM GOWERS
26								
27								
28								
29			LORD PASSFIELD					
1930	LABOUR	RAMSAY MACDONALD						
31			J. H. THOMAS		DONALD CAMERON	STEWART SYMES	JOSEPH BYRNE	
32	NATIONAL COALITION		PHILLIP CUNLIFFE-LISTER	JOHN MAFFEY				BERNARD BOURDILLON
33								
34						HAROLD MACMICHAEL		
35	CONSERVATIVE	STANLEY BALDWIN	M. MACDONALD		BERNARD BOURDILLON			
36			J. H. THOMAS					
37			W. ORMSBY-GORE	C. PARKINSON			ROBERT BROOKE-POPHAM	CHARLES DUNDAS
38		NEVILLE CHAMBERLAIN		G. GATER				
1939			M. MACDONALD			MARK YOUNG		

Appendix 2

Biographies of Selected British Administrators

(Compiled from Colonial Office Staff Lists,
The Dictionary of National Biography, and Who Was Who)

Cyril Wilson Alexander, C.M.G.
   Born 1879. Educated Shrewsbury and Trinity College,
   Cambridge, B.A., LL.B. Assistant District Commissioner,
   Southern Nigeria, 1906; Junior Assistant Secretary, 1908;
   Acting Police Magistrate, 1908. Commissioner of Lands,
   Lagos, 1908; 2nd-class Resident, 1919; Acting Secretary,
   Northern Provinces, 1924; Acting Principal Assistant
   Secretary, Northern Provinces, 1925; Staff grade, 1925.
   Acting Lt. Governor, Northern Nigeria, 1927; Lt. Gover-
   nor, Southern Nigeria, 1929; Lt. Governor, Northern
   Nigeria, 1930. Retired 1932. Died 1947.

Sir (Henry) Hesketh (Joujou) Bell, K.C.M.G.
   Born 1865. Educated in Paris. Colonial Service in the
   West Indies, the Gold Coast, the Bahamas, and again in
   the West Indies, 1882-1906. Governor of Uganda, 1906-09.
   Governor of Northern Nigeria, 1909-12. Governor of the
   Leeward Islands, 1912-15. Governor of Mauritius, 1915-
   24. Died 1952.

Sir Bernard (Henry) Bourdillon, G.C.M.G., K.B.E.
   Born 1883. Educated at Tonbridge School and St. John's
   College, Oxford. Served in the Indian Civil Service,
   1908-14. Seconded to Mesopotamia, 1914-19, and on political duty in Iraq until 1929. Chief Secretary, Ceylon,
   1929-32. Governor of Uganda, 1932-35. Governor of
   Nigeria, 1935-43. Died 1948.

Sir Walter Buchanan-Smith, C.M.G., M.C.
   Born 1879. Educated Repton School. British North
   Borneo Civil Service, 1903; Assistant District Commis-
   sioner, Southern Nigeria, 1909; Acting Commissioner of
   Lands, Nigeria, 1912, 1914, and 1916. Attached Nigeria
   Regiment in Cameroons 1914-15 and in East Africa 1916-
   18. 1st-class District Officer, Southern Nigeria, 1918;
   Resident, 1921; Acting Principal Assistant Secretary,
   Southern Provinces, 1921, 1923, and 1925; Acting Secre-
   tary, Southern Provinces, 1923 and 1925; Staff grade,

1926; Acting Lt. Governor, Southern Provinces, 1930.
Officer Administering Government, Nigeria, Sept.-Nov.
1930.

Sir Alan Burns, G.C.M.G.
Born 9 November 1887. Educated St. Edmunds College,
Ware. Colonial Service, Leeward Islands, 1905-12;
Nigeria, 1912-24; Colonial Secretary, Bahamas, 1924-29.
Administered Bahamas parts of years 1924-28. Deputy
Chief Secretary, Nigeria, 1929-34. Governor of British
Honduras, 1934-40. Assistant Undersecretary of State
for Colonies, 1940-41. Governor of the Gold Coast,
1941-47; Acting Governor, Nigeria, 1942. Permanent
United Kingdom Representative of Trusteeship Council,
U.N., 1947-56; Chairman, Committee on Land and Popula-
tion Problems, Fiji, 1950.

Sir Horace Byatt, G.C.M.G.
Born 22 March 1875. Educated Lincoln College, Oxford,
B.A. Assistant Collector, Nyassaland Protectorate, 1899-
1905. Assistant Political Officer, Somaliland, 1905-
16; Secretary to Administration, 1906-10; Commissioner
and Commander in Chief, Somaliland, 1911-14. Colonial
Secretary, Gibraltar, 1914. Lt. Governor and Chief
Secretary, Malta, 1914-16. Administrator of conquered
territory East Africa, 1916-20; Governor of Tanganyika
Territory 1920-24. Governor of Trinidad and Tobago,
1924-29. Died 8 April 1933.

Sir Charles C. Dundas, K.C.M.G., O.B.E.
Born 6 June 1884, Fifth son of Viscount Melville. Educat-
ed on the Continent. Assistant District Commissioner,
British East Africa Protectorate, 1908-14; District
Commissioner, Kenya, 1914; Political Officer, East Africa,
1914-20; Senior Commissioner, Tanganyika Territory,
1920-24; Assistant Chief Secretary, 1924; Secretary for
Native Affairs, 1926-28; and Acting Chief Secretary,
Tanganyika, 1926. Colonial Secretary, Bahamas, 1929-34;
Acting Governor, Bahamas, various times after 1929.
Chief Secretary, Northern Rhodesia, 1934-37. Governor
of Bahamas, 1937-40. Governor of Uganda, 1940-44. Re-
tired 1945.

Sir William Egerton, C.M.G.
Born 1858. Educated Tonbridge School. Cadet, Straits
Settlements, Oct. 1880; Magistrate, Singapore, 1881;
passed Malay, May 1882; Collector of Land Revenue,
Penang, 1883; Second Magistrate of Police, Penang, May

138

1883; Acting Senior District Officer, Butterwork P.W.,
April 1890; Justice of Peace and Coroner, Straits
Settlements, July 1893; Registrar of Deeds, Singapore,
June 1896; Inspector of Prisons, May 1897; First Magis-
trate of Penang, April 1897, of Singapore, Oct. 1898;
Acting Colonial Secretary of State, April 1900; Acting
Colonial Treasurer, Straits Settlements, Aug.-Oct. 1902.
High Commissioner to Southern Nigeria, Nov. 1903.

Col. Sir (Edward) Percy Girouard, K.C.M.G., D.S.O.
Born 1867. Served in the Royal Engineers, Sudan. Dir-
ector of Railways, Egypt and South Africa. High Commis-
sioner, then Governor, Northern Nigeria, 1907-09.
Governor of the East African Protectorate, 1909-12.
Died 1932.

Sir William (Frederick) Gowers, K.C.M.G.
Born 1875. Educated at Rugby and Trinity College,
Cambridge. Served in the British South African Company,
Southern Rhodesia, 1899-1902. Resident, Yola, Muri,
Sokoto, Bauchi, and Kano, 1903-12; Acting Chief Secre-
tary, 1912. Served in the Cameroons, 1914-16. Lt.
Governor, Southern Provinces, 1921-25. Governor of
Uganda, 1925-32. Senior Crown Agent, 1932-38. Died
1954.

Sir Selwyn MacGregor Grier, K.C.M.G.
Born 1878. Educated at Marlborough College and Pembroke
College, Cambridge, B.A. 1900 (Classics). Called to
the bar, Nov. 1910. Schoolmaster at Berkhamsted, Herts,
1901-02, and at Cheam, Surrey, 1902-05. Assistant
Resident, Northern Nigeria, 1906; passed in Hausa, 1907;
3rd-class Resident, Oct. 1908; in charge of Zaria Province, April 1910 and from May-Nov. 1911. Secretary
for Native Affairs, Nigeria, Jan. 1921. Colonial Secretary, Trinidad, 1929-35. Governor of the Windward Islands, 1935-37. Died 1945.

Major-General Sir Philip Mitchell, G.C.M.G., M.C.
Born 1 May 1890. Educated, privately, St. Pauls School;
Trinity College, Oxford. Assistant Resident, Nyasaland,
1912; Lieutenant, K.A.R., 1915, Captain, 1917, Adjutant,
1917-18; A.D.C. and private secretary to Governor of
Nyasaland, 1918-19. Assistant Political Officer, Tanganyika Territory, 1919-26; Assistant Secretary
Affairs, Tanganyika, 1926-28; Provincial Commissioner,
1928; Secretary of Native Affairs, Tanganyika Territory,
1928-34; Chief Secretary, 1934-35. Governor of Uganda,

1935-40. Deputy Chairman of Conference of East African
Governors, 1940. Political Advisor to General Sir
Archibald Wavell, 1941; Plenipotentiary in Ethiopia and
Chief Political Officer to G.O.C. East Africa, 1942.
Governor of Fiji and High Commissioner for Western Paci-
fic, 1942-44. Governor of Kenya, 1944-52.

Sir Ralph Denham Rayment Moor, K.C.M.G.
Born 1860. Educated privately. Learner in tea trade,
1880-81. Entered Royal Irish Constabulary as a cadet;
rose to position of District Inspector; resigned Feb.
1891. Entered service in Nigeria under Sir Claude Mac-
Donald, March 1891. Appointed Deputy Commissioner and
Vice-Consul in Oil Rivers Protectorate and adjoining
native territory, July 1892; acting administrator and
Consul General, Aug. 1892-Feb. 1893, April 1894-Nov.
1894, and July-Dec. 1895; appointed Consul in Jan. 1896.
Commissioner and Consul General, Niger Coast Protectorate and adjoining native territories; Consul in Cameroons
and to Fernando Po in Jan. 1896. Appointed High Commissioner for Southern Nigeria, 1900. Retired because of
health, Oct. 1903. Died 1904.

Lt. Col. Harry Claude Moorhouse, C.M.G., D.S.O., officer of
Legion of Honor. Entered Royal Artillery, 1891; Captain,
1899; Major, 1902, temporary Lt. Col., 1914. Served in
Uganda, 1898; West Africa, 1900; Southern Nigeria, 1901-
02; Northern Nigeria, 1903; Southern Nigeria, 1904
(D.S.O.). Chief Assistant Colonial Secretary, Southern
Nigeria, 1908; Secretary, Southern Provinces, 1 Jan.
1914; Lt. Governor, Nigeria, 1 Jan. 1920.

Sir Herbert Richmond Palmer, C.M.G., C.B.E.
Born 1877. Educated Oundle School and Trinity Hall,
Cambridge, M.A., LL.B.. Barrister-at-law, Middle Temple
1904. Assistant Resident, Northern Nigeria, Oct. 1904;
Commissioner of Native Revenue, Northern Nigeria, 1911;
revenue mission to Anglo-Egyptian Sudan 1912; supervisor,
native revenue, Nigeria, 1914; Acting Resident, Kano
Province, 1915-16; Resident, Bornu Province, 1917. Visit-
ed the Anglo-Egyptian Sudan from Bornu via Wadai and
Darfur, 1918. Acting Lt. Governor, Northern Nigeria,
May-Dec. 1921; Acting Resident Sokoto Province, April-
May 1922; Lt. Governor, Northern Nigeria, May 1925.
Governor of the Gambia, 1930-33. Governor of Cyprus,
1933-39. Died 1958.

Major Upton Fitzherbert Ruxton, C.M.G.
Born 1873. Assistant Resident, Nigeria, Feb. 1901;

2nd-class Resident, Oct. 1902; 1st-class Resident, Oct.
1908. Seconded to Admiralty, April 1916 to May 1919.
Seconded to Foreign Office for Political Duties, Con-
stantinople, May 1919. Returned to Nigeria, Aug. 1921;
Lt. Governor, Southern Provinces, Oct. 1925-March 1929.
Died 1954.

Sir John Scott, K.B.E., C.M.G.
Born 24 April 1878. Educated Leeds Grammar School;
Bath College; Kings College, Cambridge. Ceylon Civil
Service, 1901-21. Deputy Chief Secretary, Nigeria,
1921-24; Chief Secretary, Tanganyika Territory, 1924-
29. Colonial Secretary, Straits Settlements, 1929.
Retired 1929. Died Jan. 1946.

Sir Bryan (Evers) Sharwood-Smith, K.C.M.G., K.C.V.O., K.B.E.,
E.D.
Born 1899. Educated at Aldenham School. Served in the
Royal Flying Corps in World War I and in Germany and
India. Served in the Cameroons, 1921-27, and in Sokoto,
1940-42. Resident, Niger, Sokoto, and Kano, 1943-52,
and Acting Chief Commissioner, 1950. Lt. Governor and
later Governor of Northern Nigeria, 1952-57.

Sir Graeme Thomson, K.C.M.G.
Born 1875. Educated Winchester and New College, Oxford.
Higher division clerk in Admiralty, 1900. Assistant
Director of Transport, 1914; Director of Transport,
1914. Colonial Secretary of Ceylon, Sept. 1919; officer
administrating Government, 8-18 Jan. 1920 and Mar.-Sept.
1920. Governor and Commander in Chief, Nigeria, 1925.
Appointed Governor of Ceylon 1930, but died before assum-
ing position.

George John Frederick Tomlinson
B.A. Oxford. Barrister-at-law, Inner Temple. Served
in education department, Transvaal, Feb. 1903-Oct. 1904.
Assistant Resident, Northern Nigeria, July 1907. Seconded to Gold Coast as Director of Education, Dec. 1909-
Dec. 1910. 3rd-class Resident, Northern Nigeria, April
1911; Assistant Secretary for Native Affairs, Nigeria,
Jan. 1921. Transferred to Colonial Office, 1928. Assistant Undersecretary of State, 1930-39. Died 1963.

Notes

1: Early Career and Nigerian Developments

1. Sir Donald Cameron, <u>My Tanganyika Service and Some Nigeria</u> (London: Allen and Unwin, 1939).

2. The only detailed sources for Cameron's early life are the short biography in <u>Who Was Who</u>, 1941-1950, vol. 4 (London: Adam and Charles Black, 1952), Sir Alan Burns' article in L. G. W. Legg and E. T. Williams (eds.), <u>The Dictionary of National Biography, 1941-1950</u> (Oxford, 1959), p. 132, and the details contained in the Colonial Office <u>Staff List</u> for the years of Cameron's active service. There are small bits of information in Sir Philip Mitchell, <u>African Afterthoughts</u> (London: Hutchinson, 1954), pp. 103-106. All descriptions of Cameron's early career have been supplemented by discussions with and letters from persons who knew and served with him.

3. Mitchell, <u>African Afterthoughts</u>, p. 104.

4. Comment by Gerald S. Sayers in letter of remembrance to author, 3 November 1971.

5. Boyle to Lord Elgin, 3 June 1907, C. O. 167/779.

6. Mitchell, <u>African Afterthoughts</u>, p. 105.

7. <u>Ibid</u>., p. 106.

8. Lord Altrincham (Sir Edward Grigg), <u>Kenya's Opportunity</u> (London: Faber and Faber, 1955), p. 202.

9. Burns, <u>Dictionary of National Biography</u>, p. 132.

10. Statements from interview with J. J. Tawney, 26 August 1971, interview with Dr. Anthony Sillery, 7 September 1971, and long letter from G. S. Sayers to author, 3 November 1971.

11. Judith Listowel, <u>The Making of Tanganyika</u> (New York: London House and Maxwell, 1965), p. 95.

12. Letter from J. Rooke Johnston to author, 20 December 1971.

13. Letter from G. S. Sayers to author, 15 December 1971, and interview with J. J. Tawney, 26 August 1971.

14. Telegram from Bower to Colonial Office, 24 July 1907, C. O. 167/779.

15. Minute by Lucas to Sir Francis Hopwood, 26 August 1907, Ibid.

16. Minutes by Lucas and Stubbs, 3 October 1907, Ibid.

17. Cameron, My Tanganyika Service and Some Nigeria, pp. 261-263.

18. The best volume on the Yoruba in the nineteenth century and British expansion in the West is Samuel Johnson, The History of the Yorubas, (Lagos, C. M. S. Bookshops, 1921). See also G. J. A. Ojo, Yoruba Culture (London: University of London Press, 1967), and J. F. Ade Ajayi and Robert Smith, Yoruba Warfare in the 19th Century (London: Cambridge University Press, 1964).

19. J. C. Anene, Southern Nigeria in Transition, 1885-1906 (London: Cambridge University Press, 1966).

20. For generalized treatment of British expansion in the North see Margery Perham, Lugard, Years of Authority, 1899-1945 (London: Collins, 1960) and D. J. Muffet, Concerning Brave Captains (London: A. Deutsch, 1964).

2: Deputy to Lugard and Clifford

1. Cameron, My Tanganyika Service and Some Nigeria, pp. 153-154.

2. Perham, Lugard, Years of Authority, p. 619.

3. Ibid., pp. 364-365.

4. Cmd. 468, Report by Sir F. D. Lugard on the Amalgamation of Northern and Southern Nigeria and Administration, 1912-1919.

5. C. O. 583/9.

6. Perham, Lugard, Years of Authority, pp. 476-485. For Temple's written rebuttal to those items he considered wrong see Charles L. Temple, Native Races and Their Rulers (London: Frank Cass, 1968).

7. Perham, Lugard, Years of Authority, pp. 616-617.

8. The best treatment of the early systems of British rule and the implications of Lugard's changes are in Anene, Southern Nigeria in Transition and A. E. Afigbo, The Warrant Chiefs: Indirect Rule in Southeastern Nigeria (New York: Humanities Press, 1972).

9. For Lugard's opinion on the subject of anthropologists see his speech to the Legislative Council, 12 March 1914, in C. O. 583/10.

10. Native Courts Ordinance No. 8, 1914.

11. Provincial Courts Ordinance No. 3, 1914.

12. Native Authority Ordinance, 1916.

13. Perham, Native Administration in Nigeria (London: Oxford University Press, 1937), p. 72.

14. Cmd. 468. Appendix ii contains the treaty with the Alake. Lugard's reasons for such action are contained in paragraph 19. Clifford's disagreement with this policy is found in Clifford to Milner, 9 April 1920, C. O. 583/85.

15. There are few accounts of the fighting near Abeokuta. The Colonial Office sponsored an investigation but never published the results. For the most detailed current reports see West Africa, 17 and 24 August 1918, and 31 January and 7 March 1925.

16. For the details of the women's disturbances see Harry A. Gailey, The Road to Aba (New York: New York University Press, 1971).

17. Perham, Lugard, Years of Authority, pp. 577-578.

18. Ibid., p. 609.

19. Sir Alan Burns, Colonial Civil Servant (London: George Allen and Unwin, 1949), p. 54.

20. Clifford to Milner, Confidential, 26 May 1920, C. O. 583/88.

21. The most scathing indictment of Lugard's amalgamation

plan and lack of necessary administrative forms is in
I. F. Nicolson, The Administration of Nigeria, 1900-
1960 (Oxford: Clarendon Press, 1969), pp. 180-215.

22. Cameron, My Tanganyika Service and Some Nigeria, p. 142.

23. Conversation with Dame Margery Perham, 7 September 1971.

24. Basic details of Clifford's life are taken from The Dictionary of National Biography and from the Colonial
Office Staff List.

25. R. E. Wraith, Guggisberg (London: Oxford University
Press, 1967), pp. 73-97.

26. Nicolson, The Administration of Nigeria, pp. 219-237.

27. Report of Salaries Commision, 17 February 1920, C. O.
583/84.

28. Clifford to Churchill, 1 January 1922, C. O. 583/108.

29. Clifford to Milner, 3 December 1919, C. O. 583/80.

30. Clifford to Milner, Confidential, 26 May 1920, C. O.
583/88.

31. Ibid.

32. Clifford to Milner, Confidential, 9 December 1920, C. O.
583/94.

33. Temple, Native Races and their Rulers, p. 240.

34. Burns, Colonial Civil Servant, p. 47.

35. Minute dated 16 February 1922, C. O. 583/108.

36. Cameron, My Tanganyika Service and Some Nigeria, p. 150.

37. For example see Cameron's handling of the Eleko Affair,
C. O. 583/101.

38. Sir Donald Cameron, "Native Administration in Nigeria
and Tanganyika," Journal of the Royal African Society,
vol. 36 (30 November 1937), p. 10.

39. Cameron, My Tanganyika Service and Some Nigeria, p. 17.

40. Clifford to Milner, Confidential, 24 June 1920, C. O. 583/89.

41. Minute by A. J. Herbert dated 21 June 1921, C. O. 583/89.

42. Clifford to Milner, Confidential dispatch, 18 March 1920, C. O. 583/85, and Nigerian Pioneer, 9 April 1920.

43. Minute by Sir George Fiddes, 31 June 1920, C. O. 583/85.

44. Lugard to Harcourt, 10 August 1914, C. S. O. 9/1/8.

45. G. J. F. Tomlinson, Report of a Tour of the Eastern Provinces by the Assistant Secretary for Native Affairs (Lagos: Government Printer, 1923).

46. G. J. F. Tomlinson, Report of a Tour of the Eastern Provinces by the Assistant Secretary for Native Affairs (Lagos: Government Printer, 1923).

47. Memorandum by Sir Harry Moorhouse dated August 1924, C. S. O. 26/2, File 17720, vol. 1, p. 3.

48. Gailey, The Road to Aba, pp. 80-81.

49. Cameron, My Tanganyika Service and Some Nigeria, p. 17.

50. Ibid., p. 17.

51. Ibid., p. 16.

3: Tanganyika Backgrounds

1. For the East African campaign see General Paul von Lettow-Vorbeck, My Reminiscences of East Africa (London: Hurst and Blackett, 1920) and W. K. Hancock, Smuts, The Sanguine Years (London: Cambridge University Press, 1962).

2. Tanganyika Order in Council, July 1920, Tanganyika Territory: Ordinances, Proclamations, etc., vol. 1 (London: Waterlow, 1921) and League of Nations, "Council Nineteenth Session," Official Journal, 3 (Annex 374C, August 1922): 861.

3. For final approval of the Belgian treaty see League of Nations, "Council, Eighty-eighth Session, third meeting," Official Journal, 16 (November 1935): 1148, and for the Portuguese treaty see League of Nations, "Council, Ninety-eighth Session, second meeting," Official Journal, 18 (December 1937): 898.

4.   The best statement of Britain's position is that given
      by Amery on 16 August 1926 to the Tanganyika European
      Civil Servants who were afraid of a transfer of the
      territory to Germany, in C. O. 691/84.

5.   The sentiment for some type of reversion of Tanganyika
      to Germany became particularly strong after 1926. An
      example of the arguments of the German Colonial Society
      is in an article in the Duetsche Allgemeine Zeitung, 18
      June 1926. Key correspondence between this society and
      the British Foreign Office is in C. O. 691/93. For
      some idea of settler fears see editorial in East Africa,
      15 April 1926.

6.   "General Bulletin of the Imperial Institute," Berlin,
      cited in Hugh W. Stephens, The Political Transformation
      of Tanganyika, 1920-1967 (New York: Praeger, 1968),
      p. 21.

7.   S. H. Frankel, Capital Investment in Africa (London:
      Oxford University Press, 1937), p. 277.

8.   C. O. 691/78. This also contains Cameron's dispatch
      of 10 July 1925 whereby he notified his superiors that
      he was ending restrictions on German immigration and
      residence.

9.   The most detailed account of the rebellion is in Gustav
      Adolf von Gotzen, Deutsch-Ostafrika im Aufstand, 1905-
      1906 (Berlin: 1909).

10.   J. Clagett Taylor, The Political Development of Tangan-
      yika (London: Oxford University Press, 1963), pp. 20-
      21.

11.   C. O. 691/84.

12.   Native Authority Ordinance, 1921, and Native Authority
      Ordinance No. 25, 1923 in Tanganyika Territory: Ordin-
      ances, Proclamations, etc. in C. O. 735.

13.   Cmd. 2387, Report of the East Africa Commission (1925)
      (Ormsby-Gore Report).

14.   Cameron, My Tanganyika Service and Some Nigeria, p. 89.

15.   Ralph A. Austen, Northwest Tanzania under German and
      British Rule: Colonial Policy and Tribal Politics,

1889-1939 (New Haven, Yale University Press, 1968), pp. 150-151.

16. For further details of the white settlers' position see C. W. Hobley, Kenya from Chartered Company to Crown Colony (London: Witherby, 1929) and Elspeth Huxley, White Man's Country, 2 vols. (London: Macmillan, 1935).

17. Cmd. 1922, Indians in Kenya (1923).

18. The Covenant of the League is reprinted in a number of sources. See for example the Appendix to Alfred Zimmern, The League of Nations and the Rule of Law (London: Macmillan, 1939).

19. Leopold S. Amery, My Political Life, vol. 2 (London: Hutchinson, 1953) pp. 360-361.

20. See for example Winston Churchill's dispatch of 18 August 1922 in C. O. 691/83.

21. Proceedings of the Third East African Unofficial Conference (Nairobi: reprinted by East African Standard, 13 August 1927), p. 7.

22. Robert Gregory, Sidney Webb and East Africa: Labour's Experiment with the Doctrine of Native Paramountcy (Berkeley: University of California Press, 1962), p. 57.

23. Cmd. 2387, Report of the East Africa Commission (1925).

24. Basic details of Amery's career are taken from Amery, My Political Life and The Dictionary of National Biography.

25. Altrincham, Kenya's Opportunity, p. 71.

26. Ibid., p. 213.

27. Ibid., pp. 210-216. Altrincham clearly hints at Cameron's ignorance of Colonial Office intentions. This is confirmed by Cameron's dispatch to Amery, 3 May 1926, C. O. 691/84.

4: The Closer Union Controversy

1. Austen, Northwest Tanzania Under German and British Rule,

p. 153, and Cameron, <u>My Tanganyika Service and Some Nigeria</u>, p. 125.

2. Cameron, <u>My Tanganyika Service and Some Nigeria</u>, pp. 22-23.

3. Listowel, <u>The Making of Tanganyika</u>, p. 82.

4. Details of Cameron's reasoning early in his tenure are contained in his dispatch to Amery, 29 July 1925, C. O. 691/78. For changes in Royal Instructions, June 1926, see C. O. 691/86.

5. Cameron's speech to the opening of the Legislative Council, 7 December 1926 in Great Britain, Colonial No. 32, <u>Report of His Majesty's Government to the Council of the League of Nations for the Administration of Tanganyika Territory, 1927</u> (London: H.M.S.O., 1928), p. 6.

6. Letter from G. S. Sayers to author, 3 November 1971.

7. Correspondence for and the decisions to improve the harbor are in C. O. 691/85.

8. Telegram from Strachey to Cameron, 13 April 1926, C. O. 691/83.

9. C. O. 691/83.

10. Letter from Sir Rex Surridge to author, 4 December 1971. Most of the retired colonial servants, contacted by the author, who had served with Cameron were in substantial agreement concerning Cameron's habits and the influence he had on his subordinate personnel. For published confirmation see Mitchell, <u>African Afterthoughts</u>, p. 105.

11. Mitchell, <u>African Afterthoughts</u>, p. 125.

12. <u>Conference of Governors of the East African Dependencies, Summary of Proceedings, 1926</u> (London: Waterlow, 1926), pp. 40-41.

13. Cameron, <u>My Tanganyika Service and Some Nigeria</u>, p. 126.

14. <u>Ibid</u>., pp. 132-133.

15. <u>Ibid</u>., p. 125.

16. Report by Major G. St. J. Orde-Browne, O.B.E. on Labour in Tanganyika Territory with a Covering Despatch from the Governor, Colonial No. 19 (1926).

17. Cameron, My Tanganyika Service and Some Nigeria, p. 134.

18. Conference of Governors ... 1926, p. 15.

19. Ibid., p. 19.

20. Ibid. and Cameron, My Tanganyika Service and Some Nigeria, p. 126.

21. Cameron to Amery, Confidential dispatch, 25 February 1926, C. O. 691/83.

22. Lord Cranworth's speech, 13 April 1926, to Royal Colonial Institute, C. O. 691/83.

23. Churchill to Byatt, 18 August 1922, quoted in Strachey's memo, 3 May 1926, C. O. 691/83.

24. Ibid.

25. Cameron to Amery, Confidential dispatch, 3 May 1926, C. O. 691/84.

26. Grigg to "My Dear Leo," 11 June 1926, C. O. 691/84.

27. Cameron, My Tanganyika Service and Some Nigeria, p. 85.

28. Grigg to "My Dear Leo," 11 June 1926, C. O. 691/84.

29. Ibid.

30. See Ibid. and Altrincham, Kenya's Opportunity, p. 202.

31. Minute by W. A. Ormsby-Gore, 31 May 1926, C. O. 691/84.

32. Altrincham, Kenya's Opportunity, p. 212.

33. Cameron to Amery, Confidential dispatch, 29 June 1926, C. O. 691/86.

34. Perham, Lugard, Years of Authority, pp. 678-680.

35. Proceedings of the Second East African Unofficial Conference (Nairobi: Government Printers, 1926).

36. Perham, Lugard, Years of Authority, p. 680, and Cameron, My Tanganyika Service and Some Nigeria, pp. 224-227.

37. Perham, Lugard, Years of Authroity, p. 680.

38. Cameron, My Tanganyika Service and Some Nigeria, p. 86.

39. Letter from Lugard to his wife, 15 June 1927, quoted in Perham, Lugard, Years of Authority, p. 681.

40. Cmd. 2904, Future Policy in Regard to Eastern Africa (London: H.M.S.O.)., 1927).

41. Altrincham, Kenya's Opportunity, p. 216.

42. Proceedings of the Third East African Unofficial Conference.

43. Cmd. 3234, Report on the Commission on Closer Union of the Dependencies in Eastern and Central Africa (London: H.M.S.O. 1929).

44. For Delamere's reactions to the Hilton Young report see telegram from Delamere to Grigg, 30 January 1929 in Altrincham, Kenya's Opportunity, Appendix F, pp. 271-273.

45. Amery, My Political Life, vol. 2, pp. 361-362.

46. Altrincham, Kenya's Opportunity, p. 213.

47. Cmd. 3378, Report by Sir Samuel Wilson, G.C.M.G. on His Visit to East Africa (London: H.M.S.O.)., 1929).

48. Details of the Moshi meeting are in Cameron to Passfield, Confidential dispatch, 16 August 1929, C. O. 691/106.

49. Cameron, My Tanganyika Service and Some Nigeria, p. 120.

50. Mitchell, African Afterthoughts, p. 117.

51. Cameron to Amery, 10 May 1929 and Passfield to Cameron, 13 January 1930, C. O. 691/106.

52. Mitchell, African Afterthoughts, p. 117.

53. Cameron to Passfield, 16 August 1929, and Wilson's minute to this dispatch, C. O. 691/106.

54. Cmd. 3574, Statement of the Conclusions of His Majesty's Government in the United Kingdom as Regards Closer Union in East Africa (London: H.M.S.O. 1930).

55. Letter from Sir John Nicoll to author, 9 May 1972.

56. Mitchell, African Afterthoughts, pp. 117-118.

5: Revision of Tanganyika Local Government

1. Cameron, My Tanganyika Service and Some Nigeria, p. 20.

2. Tanganyika Territory, Ordinance No. 12 of 1922, Hut and Poll Tax Ordinance.

3. Byatt to Colonial Office, 27 March 1924, C. O. 691/69.

4. Cameron, My Tanganyika Service and Some Nigeria, p. 175.

5. Cameron to Amery, 31 December 1925, C. O. 691/83.

6. Figures taken from Cmd. 4182, Report by Sir S. Armitage-Smith on a Financial Mission to Tanganyika (London: H. M.S.O., 1932), p. 27.

7. Margaret Bates, "Tanganyika Under British Administration, 1920-1955," (D. Phil. dissertation, Oxford University, 1957), p. 116.

8. Cameron, My Tanganyika Service and Some Nigeria, pp. 89-90.

9. Sir Donald Cameron, Principles of Native Administration and their Application (Dar es Salaam: Government Printers, 1930), p. 7.

10. Robert Heussler, British Tanganyika (Durham, N.C.: Duke University Press, 1971), p. 47.

11. Cameron, My Tanganyika Service and Some Nigeria, p. 33.

12. Heussler in British Tanganyika, pp. 46-54 does an excellent job of illustrating the shortcomings of Cameron's system. Also see Bates, "Tanganyika Under British Administration," p. 87.

13. The best statements of the role of the Secretary for

153

Native Affairs are Governor Symes to Secretary of State 6 March 1932 in Cmd. 4141, Correspondence (1931-32) Arising from the Report of the Joint Committee of Parliament on Closer Union in East Africa (1932), pp. 44-45, and Mitchell, African Afterthoughts, pp. 132-133.

14. Opinions of district officers concerning Cameron were related to the author by Dr. Anthony Sillery on 7 September 1971, J. J. Tawney on 26 August 1971, and letters from G. S. Sayers, 3 November 1971 and Sir Rex Surridge, 4 December 1971.

15. Native Authority Ordinances, 1923 and 1926 in Tanganyika Territory, Ordinances, Proclamations, etc. in C. O. 735.

16. Bates, "Tanganyika Under British Administration," pp. 91-92.

17. See particularly J. J. Tawney's account as cited in Heussler, British Tanganyika, p. 52.

18. Tanganyika Territory, Tanganyika Gazette (Supplement), 16 October 1925, p. 133.

19. Tanganyika Territory, Government Notice No. 10, Tanganyika Gazette (Supplement), January 1927.

20. Great Britain, Colonial Report, Annual, Tanganyika, 1929, p. 10.

21. Mitchell, African Afterthoughts, p. 127.

22. Statement by Mitchell on the 1928 Mwanza Province Annual Report, 28 February 1929 quoted in Austen, Northwest Tanzania Under German and British Rule, p. 156.

23. Great Britain, Colonial Report, Annual, Tanganyika, 1929, p. 11.

24. Mitchell, African Afterthoughts, p. 133.

25. See Austen, Northwest Tanzania Under German and British Rule, pp. 158-178 for a thorough treatment of Cameron's reforms in Bukoba.

26. Bates, "Tanganyika Under British Administration," p. 87.

27. Heussler, British Tanganyika, pp. 46-54.

28. For criticism of Cameron's coastal policy see Mitchell, African Afterthoughts, p. 133. This is confirmed by interview with Dr. A. Sillery, 7 September 1971 and a long letter from J. Rooke Johnston to author, 20 December 1971.

29. Mitchell, African Afterthoughts, p. 105.

30. The arguments of Rusell and Cameron are in File 18087 in C. O. 691/88.

31. Figures taken from Listowel, The Making of Tanganyika, p. 112.

32. Cameron, My Tanganyika Service and Some Nigeria, p. 117.

33. For an amplification of Cameron's relationship with the education system see Listowel, The Making of Tanganyika, pp. 85-104.

34. Conversation with Dame Margery Perham, 7 September 1971.

35. League of Nations, Permanent Mandates Commission Minutes, 22nd Session (1932), p. 131.

36. Cameron, My Tanganyika Service and Some Nigeria, pp. 102-103.

37. Ibid., p. 114.

38. Ibid., p. 115.

6: Nigerian Developments, 1924-1931

1. Cameron, My Tanganyika Service and Some Nigeria, p. 278.

2. Ibid., p. 279.

3. Ibid., pp. 25-26.

4. Ibid., p. 282.

5. Ibid., p. 290.

6. Ibid., p. 233.

7. Gailey, The Road to Aba, pp. 75-96. For the warnings of Adams, Talbot, and other district officers see Circular

of Acting Lieutenant-Governor, 2 December 1925, Nigerian Archives, Ibadan, Chief Secretary's Office (C. S. O.) 26/2, File 17720, p. 3.

8. Draft Tax Ordinance, C. S. O. 26/2, File 17720, pp. 19-23.

9. Palmer to Ruxton, 2 October 1926, C. S. O. 26/2, pp. 108-112, and minute by Alexander, 29 September 1926, C. S. O. 26/2, pp. 115-119.

10. Minute by Tomlinson, 5 November 1926, C. S. O. 26/2, pp. 136-148.

11. Nigeria Government, Gazette, 10 March 1927.

12. C. S. O. 26/2, File 20646, p. 11.

13. See C. S. O. 26/2, File 20610/6, p. 16, and 20610/4, pp. 9-10 for examples of the Assessment Reports.

14. C. S. O. 26/2, File 18417, vol. 1, p. 79.

15. Nigerian Government, Annual Report, Southern Provinces, 1929, p. 33.

16. C. O. 657/24.

17. Gailey, The Road to Aba, pp. 97-133.

18. Nigerian Government, Legislative Council, Sessional Paper No. 28, Report of a Commission of Enquiry Appointed to Inquire into the Disturbances in Calabar and Owerri Provinces, December 1929, Appendix V and pp. 44-47.

19. Nigerian Government, Legislative Council, Sessional Paper No. 12, Report of a Commission of Enquiry Appointed to Inquire into Certain Incidents at Opobo, Abak and Utu-Ekpo in December 1929, pp. 8-14 and 62-71. See also Sessional Paper No. 28, pp. 3-8 and 73-87.

20. Cmd. 3784, Despatch from the Secretary of State . . . Regarding the Commission of Inquiry into the Disturbances at Aba and Other Places (London: H.M.S.O., 1931).

21. Nigerian Government, Peace Preservation Ordinance Number

15, 1917, and Collective Punishment Ordinance Number
20, 1915.

22. For the early rationale for the establishment of Oyo
as the Native Authority see Lugard, Political Memoranda (Lagos: 1918), p. 177. For the problems of administering Ibadan see Perham, Native Administration in
Nigeria, pp. 189-194.

23. For details of the government's position in the Eleko
Affair see Cameron's dispatch to Colonial Office, 10
June 1921, C. O. 583/101.

24. Obafemi Awolowo in his book Awo (Cambridge: Cambridge
University Press, 1960), pp. 116-121 relates the actions
of early nationalists and their frustrations because of
what they considered punitive actions by the British
authorities.

25. Cameron, My Tanganyika Service and Some Nigeria, pp.
118-119.

26. Perham, Native Administration in Nigeria, p. 330.

27. Nicolson, Administration of Nigeria, pp. 239-240.

28. Figures taken from Perham, Native Administration in
Nigeria, p. 113.

29. Ibid., p. 121.

30. For a good description of this evolvement of this loose
control system see M. E. Smith, The Kingdom of Zazzau
(London: Oxford University Press, 1960). See also
S. J. Hogben and A. H. M. Kirk-Greene, The Emirates of
Northern Nigeria (London: Oxford University Press,
1966).

31. Nigerian Government, Annual Report, Northern Provinces,
1930, p. 31.

32. Perham, Native Administration in Nigeria, p. 138. For
disturbances in 1929 and 1930 in Dikwa see Great Britain,
Colonial Office, Colonial Report, Annual, Nigeria, 1930,
p. 28.

33. Perham, Native Administration in Nigeria, pp. 152-159.

34. _Ibid._, pp. 145-148.

35. _Ibid._, p. 146.

7: The Nigerian Financial Crisis

1. Conversation between author and Dame Margery Perham, 7 September 1971.

2. Compiled from Sessional Paper No. 28, pp. 38 and 102.

3. C. S. O. 26/2, File 11930, vol. 12, p. 7.

4. Great Britain, Colonial Office, Colonial Report, Annual, Nigeria, 1930 and 1935.

5. Great Britain, Colonial Office, Colonial Report, Annual, Nigeria, 1932 and 1935.

6. Cameron to Colonial Office, December 1931, C. O. 583/181.

7. Series of Confidential dispatches concerning finances between Cameron and Colonial Office between September and December 1933. C. O. 583/193.

8. C. S. O. 26/2, File 11930, vol. 11, p. 13.

9. Cameron to Colonial Office, December 1932, C. O. 583/182.

10. For lengthy correspondence on this matter see C. O. 583/181.

11. Cameron's meeting with Cunliffe-Lister in November 1932 reported in various communications in C. O. 583/184 and C. O. 583/185.

12. Cameron to Colonial Office, March 1933, C. O. 583/190.

13. Minute by George Fiddian, 15 April 1933, C. O. 583/190.

14. Minute by Fiddian, 12 May 1933, C. O. 583/190.

15. Cameron wrote a series of long Confidential dispatches on this crisis in September 1933. These and the Colonial Office replies are in C. O. 583/193.

16. Cameron to Sir W. Cecil Bottomley, 21 December 1933, C. O. 583/196.

17. Minute paper, 1 March 1934, C. O. 583/196.

18. Revised Estimate Budget 1934, C. O. 583/201.

19. Cunliffe-Lister to Cameron, 18 May 1935, C. O. 583/202.

20. Ibid.

21. Great Britain, Colonial Office, Colonial Report, Annual, Nigeria, 1931.

22. Perham, Native Administration in Nigeria, pp. 281-287.

23. Great Britain, Colonial Office, Colonial Report, Annual, Nigeria, 1932 and 1934.

24. Perham, Native Administration in Nigeria, pp. 295-297.

25. Gailey, The Road to Aba, pp. 135-137.

26. Nigerian Government, Legislative Council, Sessional Paper No. 12, and Sessional Paper No. 28.

27. Cmd. 3784, Despatch from the Secretary of State . . . Regarding the . . . Disturbances at Aba and Other Places.

28. Memorandum by C. T. Lawrence in Sessional Paper No. 28, p. 9.

29. Nigerian Government, Gazette Extraordinary, 5 April 1933.

30. Cameron to Cunliffe-Lister, Confidential dispatch, 23 November 1933, C. O. 583/191.

31. Nigerian Government, Gazette Extraordinary, 11 November 1933.

32. Great Britain, Colonial Office, Colonial Report, Annual, Nigeria, 1934, p. 89.

33. Cameron, My Tanganyika Service and Some Nigeria, p. 110.

34. The Ordinances and Cameron's justification for his actions are in C. O. 583/177.

35. Nigerian Government, Gazette Extraordinary, 29 August 1933.

159

36. Great Britain, Colonial Office, Colonial Report, Annual, Nigeria, 1931, p. 62, and Perham, Native Administration in Nigeria, pp. 127-128.

37. Perham, Native Administration in Nigeria, p. 344.

8: Revision of Nigerian Local Government

1. This was particularly true for the assessment reports submitted between 1926 and 1928. See various files in C. S. O. 26/2, and C. S. O. 26/3 for Calabar and Owerri Provinces.

2. C. K. Meek, An Ethnographic Report upon the Peoples of Nsukka Division, Onitsha Province (Lagos: Government Printer, 1933) and Report in Social and Political Organization in the Owerri Division (Lagos: Government Printer, 1934).

3. C. S. O. 26/2, File 11930, vol. 10, 1932.

4. C. S. O. 26/2, File 11929, vol. 9, 1931, p. 11.

5. Cameron to Cunliffe-Lister, Confidential dispatch, 10 December 1931, C. O. 583/177. Robert Heussler in The British in Northern Nigeria (London: Oxford Univ. Press, 1968), pp. 61-82 presents a very detailed picture of the strained relations between Cameron and the northern officers. He tends, however, to adopt the northern viewpoint. Cameron may have been brusque or even rude to officers such as Lt. Governor Alexander, but it is obvious that those northern officers viewed themselves as being above the usual rules. One must remember that Cameron, owing to his previous long service in Nigeria, was aware of their propensities and the inadequacies of the system.

6. Cameron to Cunliffe-Lister, Confidential dispatch, 10 December 1931, C. O. 583/177.

7. Ibid.

8. Minutes to Cameron's dispatch of December 1931 dated 23 February 1932 in Ibid.

9. Cameron, My Tanganyika Service and Some Nigeria, pp. 104-105.

10. Nigerian Government, <u>Legislative Council Annual Session</u>, <u>6 March 1933, Address by His Excellency the Governor</u>, <u>Sir Donald Cameron</u> (Lagos: Government Printer, 1933), pp. 16-17.

11. <u>Ibid</u>., p. 17.

12. <u>Ibid</u>.

13. <u>Nigerian Daily Times</u>, 8 March 1933.

14. <u>Ibid</u>.

15. Cunliffe-Lister to Cameron, 1 June 1933, C. O. 583/187.

16. <u>Administrative Officers (Powers of Native Authority)</u> <u>Ordinance No. 26, 1933</u>.

17. <u>Native Authority Ordinance No. 43 of 1933</u>.

18. Perham, <u>Native Administration in Nigeria</u>, p. 246.

19. Letter by Senior Resident Findley, 10 October 1933 in C. S. O. 26/3 File 27627, vol. 2.

20. Nicolson, <u>Administration of Nigeria</u>, p. 245.

21. Sir Bryan Sharwood-Smith, <u>Recollections of British Admin-</u> <u>istration in the Cameroons and Northern Nigeria, 1921-</u> <u>1957</u>: "But Always As Friends", pp. 101-102.

22. <u>Native Courts Ordinance No. 44 of 1933</u>.

23. Perham, <u>Native Administration in Nigeria</u>, pp. 91-92.

24. Cameron, <u>My Tanganyika Service and Some Nigeria</u>, p. 202.

25. <u>Protectorate Courts Ordinance No. 45 of 1933</u>.

26. <u>Supreme Court (Amendment) Ordinance No. 46 of 1933</u>.

27. <u>West African Court of Appeal Ordinance No. 47 of 1933</u>.

28. Nigerian Government, <u>Legislative Council . . . Address</u> <u>by . . . Sir Donald Cameron</u>, 6 March 1933, p. 17.

29. Cameron, <u>My Tanganyika Service and Some Nigeria</u>, p. 203.

30. Cameron to Colonial Secretary, Confidential dispatches, 18 and 19 July 1933, C. O. 583/192.

31. C. S. O. 26/2, File 11930, vol. 11, p. 4.

32. Great Britain, Colonial Office, Colonial Report, Nigeria, 1931, pp. 5-6.

33. Telegram from Cunliffe-Lister to Cameron, 20 April 1934, C. O. 583/198.

34. Great Britain, Colonial Office, Colonial Report, Nigeria, 1934, p. 5.

35. Ibid., pp. 6-7.

36. Conversation with Dame Margery Perham, 7 September 1971.

37. Governor of Nigeria to Secretary of State, 6 December 1944 in Cmd. 6599, Proposals for the Revision of the Constitution of Nigeria (1945).

38. Cameron to Bottomley, Confidential letter, 28 September 1933, C. O. 583/191.

39. C. O. 583/198 and C. O. 583/201.

40. Nicolson, Administration of Nigeria, p. 245. For Cameron's admiration of Egerton's system see Cameron, My Tanganyika Service and Some Nigeria, pp. 150-151.

41. Sharwood-Smith, Recollections, p. 107.

EPILOGUE

1. Letter from G. S. Sayers to author, 15 December 1971.

2. Conversation with Dr. Anthony Sillery, 7 September 1971 at Oxford.

3. Letter from G. S. Sayers to author, 3 November 1971.

4. Will of Sir Donald Cameron, 8 November 1945 and codicil, February 1947, Register 170, Somerset House.

5. William Edgett Smith, "Profiles (Julius Nyerere--I),"

The New Yorker, 16 October 1971, p. 90.

6. Altrincham, Kenya's Opportunity, p. 202.

7. Mitchell, African Afterthoughts, p. 132.

8. Letter to Editor, The Times, 4 April 1961 from Dr. Anthony Sillery and Sir John Nicoll.

9. Letter from G. S. Sayers to author, 3 November 1971.

Bibliography

Documents

Great Britain: Public Record Office
    Colonial Office Papers

    Mauritius:

        C. O. 167/779, Dispatches, April-July 1907.
        C. O. 167/780, Dispatches, August-October 1907.

    Nigeria:
        C. O. 583/9, Dispatches, 1914.
        C. O. 583/80 through C. O. 583/128, Dispatches,
            1919-1924.
        C. O. 583/171 through C. O. 583/202, Dispatches,
            1930-1935.

    Tanganyika:
        C. O. 691/77 through 691/106, Dispatches, April
            1925-1929.

Federal Archives, Ibadan, Nigeria
    Chief Secretary's Office Papers

    C. S. O. 26/2, File 11930, vols. 5-12.
    C. S. O. 26/2, File 17720.
    C. S. O. 26/2, Files 20677, 20682, 20689, 20690.
    C. S. O. 26/2, Files 20610/4, 20610/6, 20621, 20634,
        20645, 20646.
    C. S. O. 26/3, File 11929, vols. 5-12.
    C. S. O. 26/3, Files 26944, 27627, 29017.
    C. S. O. 26/4, Files 28239, 28939, 30984, 31106.
    C. S. O. 9/1/18.

    Owerri Province (O. W.) 104/14 and 225/14.

    Eastern Provinces (E. P.) 3759.

Great Britain: Parliamentary Papers, Papers by Command

    Cmd. 468, Report by Sir F. D. Lugard on the Amalgama-
        tion of Northern and Southern Nigeria and
        Administration, 1912-1919. 1919.

Cmd. 1428, Reports by His Majesty's Government in Tanganyika Territory, Covering the Period from
the Conclusion of the Armistice to the End
of 1920. 1920.

Cmd. 1922, Indians in Kenya. 1923.

Cmd. 2387, Report of the East Africa Commission. 1925.

Cmd. 2744, Report by W. G. A. Ormsby-Gore on His Visit
to West Africa. 1926.

Cmd. 3234, Report of the Commission on Closer Union of
the Dependencies in Eastern and Central
Africa. 1929.

Cmd. 3378, Report by Sir Samuel Wilson, G.C.M.G.,
on His Visit to East Africa. 1929.

Cmd. 3573, Memorandum on Native Policy in East Africa.
1929.

Cmd. 3574, Statement of the Conclusions of His Majesty's
Government in the United Kingdom as Regards
Closer Union in East Africa. 1930.

Cmd. 3784, Despatch from the Secretary of State . . .
Regarding the Commission of Inquiry into the
Disturbances at Aba and Other Places. 1931.

Cmd. 4141, Correspondence (1931-32) Arising from the
Report of the Joint Committee of Parliament
on Closer Union in East Africa. 1932.

Cmd. 4182, Report by Sir S. Armitage-Smith on a Financial Mission to Tanganyika. 1932.

Cmd. 6599, Proposals for the Revision of the Constitution of Nigeria. 1945.

Great Britain: Parliamentary Debates, House of Commons

8 April 1924, Debate on Commission on Closer Union.
29 July 1926, Debate on Development Policies in East
Africa.
1 December 1926, Debate on East Africa Loan Bill.
19 July 1927, (Supply) Closer Union.
20 February 1929, (Supply) Closer Union.
11 December 1929, Debate on Policy toward Coloured Races.

Great Britian: Parliamentary Debates, House of Lords

    14 July 1920, Status of Indian and Native Labour in
       East Africa.
    20 May 1925, Report of Ormsby-Gore Commission.
    7 December 1925, East African Policy.
    13 March 1929, Report of Hilton Young Commission.
    3 July and 12 November 1930, Joint Parliamentary Com-
       mittee on Closer Union.

Great Britain: Colonial Office Publications

Colonial Reports, Annual, Nigeria. 1920-1935.
Colonial Reports, Annual, Tanganyika. 1925-1930.
Colonial No. 19, J. Orde Browne, Labour in Tanganyika
    Territory with a Covering Despatch from the Gov-
    ernor. 1926.
Colonial No. 32, Report of His Majesty's Government to
    the Council of the League of Nations for the Admin-
    istration of Tanganyika Territory, 1927. 1928.

Nigeria Government Publications

Annual Reports. 1925-1935.
Authenticated Ordinances. 1912-1935.
Gazette. 1920-1935.
Grier, S. M. Report on the Eastern Province by the
    Secretary for Native Affairs. 1922.
Legislative Council. Legislative Council Annual Session,
    6 March 1933, Address by His Excellency the Gover-
    nor, Sir Donald Cameron. 1933.
Legislative Council. Sessional Paper No. 12, Report of
    a Commission of Enquiry Appointed to Inquire into
    Certain Incidents at Opobo, Abak, and Utu-Ekpo in
    December 1929. 1930.
Legislative Council. Sessional Paper No. 28, Report of
    a Commission of Enquiry Appointed to Inquire into
    the Disturbances in Calabar and Owerri Provinces,
    December 1929. 1930.
Lugard, Lord F. D. Political Memoranda. 1918.
Tomlinson, G. J. F. Report of a Tour of the Eastern
    Provinces by the Assistant Secretary for Native
    Affairs. 1923.

Tanganyika Government Publications

Tanganyika Gazette, 1919-1930.
Blue Books for Tanganyika Territory, 1921-1930.

Tanganyika Territory: Ordinances, Proclamations, etc.
     London: Waterlow (prior to 1923) and C.O. 735
     (after 1923).
Tanganyika Territory: Proceedings of the Legislative
     Council. First Session. 1926-27.

Miscellaneous Publications

     League of Nations, Official Journal. 1922, 1935, 1937.
     _____. Permanent Mandates Commission Minutes.
     Conference of Governors of the East African Dependencies,
          Summary of Proceedings, 1926. London: Waterlow,
          1926.
     Proceedings of the Second East African Unofficial Con-
          ference. Nairobi: Government Printers, 1926.
     Proceedings of the Third East African Unofficial Confer-
          ence. Nairobi: reprinted by East African Standard,
          13 August 1927.

Unpublished Dissertations

Bates, Margaret L. "Tanganyika Under British Administration,
     1920-1955." D. Phil. dissertation, Oxford University,
     1957.

Moule, Malcolm. "The British Administration of Tanganyika."
     Ph.D. dissertation, Stanford University, 1947.

Tamuno, Tekana. "The Development of British Administrative
     Control of Southern Nigeria, 1900-1912." Ph.D. disser-
     tation, University of London, 1963.

Books

Afigbo, A. E. The Warrant Chiefs: Indirect Rule in South-
     eastern Nigeria. New York: Humanities Press, 1972.

Ajayi, J. F. Ade and Smith, Robert. Yoruba Warfare in the
     19th Century. London: Cambridge University Press,
     1964.

Altrincham, Lord (Sir Edward Grigg). Kenya's Opportunity.
     London: Faber and Faber, 1955.

Amery, Leopold S. My Political Life. 2 vols. London:
     Hutchinson, 1953.

Anene, J. C. Southern Nigeria in Transition, 1885-1906.
     London: Cambridge University Press, 1966.

Austen, Ralph A. Northwest Tanganyika Under German and British Rule: Colonial Policy and Tribal Politics, 1889-1939. New Haven: Yale University Press, 1968.

Awolowo, Obafemi. Awo. London: Cambridge University Press, 1960.

Buell, Raymond Leslie. The Native Problem in Tropical Africa. 2 vols. New York: Macmillan, 1928.

Burns, Sir Alan. Colonial Civil Servant. London: George Allen and Unwin, 1949.

Cameron, Sir Donald. My Tanganyika Service and Some Nigeria. London: Allen and Unwin, 1939.

_____. Principles of Native Administration and their Application. Dar es Salaam: Government Printer, 1930.

Chidzero, B. T. G. Tanganyika and International Trusteeship. London: Oxford University Press, 1961.

Cohen, Sir Andrew. British Policy in Changing Africa. Evanston, Ill.: Northwestern University Press, 1959.

Coleman, James S. Nigeria, Background to Nationalism. Berkeley: University of California Press, 1958.

Crowder, Michael. A Short History of Nigeria. New York: Praeger, 1962.

Dundas, Sir Charles. African Crossroads. London: Macmillan, 1955.

Gailey, Harry A. The Road to Aba. New York: New York University Press, 1970.

von Götzen, Gustav Adolf. Deutsch-Ostafrika im Aufstand, 1905-1906. Berlin: n.p., 1909.

Gregory, Robert G. Sidney Webb and East Africa: Labour's Experiment with the Doctrine of Native Paramountcy. Berkeley, University of California Press, 1962.

Hailey, Lord. Native Administration in the British African Territories. 5 vols. London: H.M.S.O., 1951-53.

Hancock, W. K. Smuts, The Sanguine Years. London: Cambridge
     University Press, 1962.

Harlow, Vincent (E. M. Chilver and Alison Smith, eds.). His-
     tory of East Africa, vol. 2. London: Oxford University
     Press, 1965.

Heussler, Robert. The British in Northern Nigeria. London:
     Oxford University Press, 1968.

_____. British Tanganyika. Durham, N.C.: Duke
     University Press, 1971.

Hobley, C. W. Kenya from Chartered Company to Crown Colony.
     London: Witherby, 1929.

Hogben, S. J. and Kirk-Greene, A. H. M. The Emirates of
     Northern Nigeria. London: Oxford University Press,
     1966.

Huxley, Elspeth. White Man's Country. 2 vols. London:
     Macmillan, 1935.

Ilife, John. Tanganyika Under German Rule. London: Cambridge
     University Press, 1969.

Ingham, Kenneth. A History of East Africa. New York:
     Praeger, 1967.

von Lettow-Vorbeck, Paul. My Reminiscences of East Africa.
     London: Hurst and Blackett, 1920.

Listowel, Judith. The Making of Tanganyika. New York:
     London House and Maxwell, 1965.

Meek, C. K. An Ethnographic Report upon the Peoples of
     Nsukka Division, Onitsha Province. Lagos: Government
     Printer, 1933.

_____. Report on Social and Political Organization in
     the Owerri Division. Lagos: Government Printer, 1934.

Mitchell, Sir Philip. African Afterthoughts. London:
     Hutchinson, 1954.

Morris-Hale, Walter. British Administration in Tanganyika
     from 1920 to 1945. Geneva: Imprime, 1969.

Muffet, D. J. Concerning Brave Captains. London: A.
    Deutsch, 1964.

Nicolson, I. F. The Administration of Nigeria, 1900-1960.
    Oxford: Clarendon Press, 1969.

Ojo, G. J. A. Yoruba Culture. London: University of London
    Press, 1967.

Oldham, J. H. New Hope for Africa. London: Longman's, 1955.

Perham, Dame Margery. Lugard, Years of Authority, 1899-1945.
    London: Collins, 1960.

_____. Native Administration in Nigeria.
    London: Oxford University Press, 1937.

Sayers, G. S. (ed.). The Handbook of Tanganyika. London:
    Macmillan, 1930.

Schacht, Hjalmar. New Colonial Policy. Berlin: Reichsbank,
    1926.

Sharwood-Smith, Sir Bryan. Recollections of British Adminis-
    tration in the Cameroons and Northern Nigeria 1921-1957:
    "But Always as Friends." Durham, N.C.: Duke University
    Press, 1969.

Smith, Michael E. The Kingdom of Zazzau. London: Oxford
    University Press, 1960.

Stephens, Hugh W. The Political Transformation of Tanganyika:
    1920-67. New York: Praeger, 1968.

Symes, Sir Stewart. Tour of Duty. London: Collins, 1946.

Taylor, J. Clagett. The Political Development of Tanganyika.
    London: Oxford University Press, 1963.

Temple, C. L. Native Races and their Rulers. London: Frank
    Cass, 1968.

Upthegrove, C. L. Empire by Mandate. New York: Bookman,
    1954.

Wraith, R. E. Guggisberg. London: Oxford University Press,
    1967.

Zimmern, Alfred. The League of Nations and the Rule of Law.
    London: Macmillan, 1939.

Index

British Conservative Party, 2, 129
British Guiana, 3, 4
British Honduras, 4
British Labour Party, 2, 31, 53, 58, 62, 65, 129
British Parliament, Joint Committee, 64-65, 86, 89
Browne, George, 118
Buchanan-Smith, Walter, 106, 118
Bukoba, 36, 38, 70, 77-78, 85, 88
Burns, Sir Alan, 6, 21, 26
Byatt, Sir Horace, 3, 31, 33, 35-36, 67, 81, 82

Catholic missions, 82
Calabar Province, 10, 93, 107, 119
Cameron, Donald Charles (Sr.), 3
Cameron, Sir Donald Charles,
    physical description, 5-6; personality, 6-7; humor, 6-7;
    marriage, 7-8; work habits, 6, 26-27, 55; early career,
    West Indies, 4-5; early career, Mauritius, 5, 8-9; early
    career, Nigeria, 9, 12, 13; slander suit, 125-126; later
    years, 129 ff.

    relations with: Leopold Amery, 44, 56 ff.; Sir Hugh
    Clifford, 24-26, 28, 30, 33; Colonial Office, 8-9, 26,
    27, 56 ff., 67, 84, 88, 104-105, 118, 125, 129; Lord
    Delamere, 56, 60, 61; Sir Edward Grigg, 52, 53-55,
    56 ff.; Lord Frederick D. Lugard, 9, 12, 16, 20, 22, 33,
    56-57, 59, 89, 124-125; Lord Passfield, 84, 87, 88, 93,
    107

    Tanganyika service: closer union, 44, 56 ff.; economic
    problems, 46, 47; education policy, 81-83; German land-
    owners, 52, 53, 64; indirect rule, 47, 60, 67 ff., 122;
    labor policy, 50-51, 63; land policy, 60, 62-64; Legis-
    lative Council, 46-47, 86, 87-88; League of Nations, 54,
    56, 58, 84; Secretariat, 48-49; white settlers, 45,
    52-53, 62-64

    Nigeria service: acting governor, 27; agriculture, 105;
    central government, 103, 116, 118-119; economic problems,
    101-105; educational system, 105-106; Eleko affair, 94-
    95, 110-111; elite, 94-95, 110; indirect rule, 27-28,
    67, 101, 103, 106-110, 113 ff.; Legislative Council, 94,
    116-118, 122, 125; Native Courts, 114, 120-123; Northern
    Nigeria, 111-112, 115-117, 120, 123-124; Provincial and
    District Officers, 107-108, 119-120; reassessment reports,
    108, 113-114; redistricting, 123-124, 127; Secretariat,
    12, 20, 24-28; taxation, 103-104; travel policy, 109-110

Cameron, Geoffrey Valentine, 8, 130
Cameron, Lady Gertrude Gittens, 7-8, 13, 57
Cameron, Mary Emily Brassington, 3
Cameroons, 34
Chagga, 36, 41, 51
Church, A. G., 42
Church Missionary Society, 131
Churchill, Winston, 41, 43, 53, 56
Clifford, Sir Hugh,
    and Cameron, 24-26, 28, 30; and Colonial Office, 25,
    29, 98; and indirect rule, 27-30, 95, 97, 98, 115-116;
    and taxation, 29-30, 89; early career, 23-24; work
    habits, 21

Collective Punishment Ordinance, 107
Commissions of Inquiry (Women's disturbances), 107
Cranworth, Lord, 52
Cunliffe-Lister, Sir Philip (Col. Sec.), 104, 115
Curtis, Lionel, 58

Dabai Emirate, 124
Dar es Salaam, 11, 34, 39, 41, 45, 47, 62, 69, 71, 77, 88,
    122
Delafield, E. M., 23
Delamere, Lord, 39, 40, 42, 56, 60, 61
de la Mothe, Mt., 62-63
de la Pasture, Mrs. Henry, 23
Demerara, 3
Devonshire, Duke of (Col. Sec.), 31, 39-40, 52
Dikwa Emirate, 98
Docemo, 94, 110
Dual Mandate, 1
Dummak tribe, 124
Duncan, Sir Patrick, 59
Dundas, Sir Charles, 49, 71, 72, 79, 80

East African Commission Report, 1924-25, 38
East African Governor's Conference, 1926, 44, 49-50, 51-52,
    53
Education Advisory Committee, 129
Efik, 114
Egba, 10, 19, 29
Egerton, Sir Walter, 10, 13, 17, 127
Eleko controversy, 94-95, 110-111
Elgin, Lord (Col. Sec.), 14
Enugu, 106
Eshugbayi, 94, 110-111

Falalu, 110-111
Fiddes, Sir George, 29
Fiddian, George, 104
Fiji, 132
Fulani, 11, 18, 35, 111, 124

Gambia, 69
Gogo, 35
Goldie, Sir George, 16
Gombolalos, 77
Gowers, Sir William, 31, 44, 45, 62
Grier, S. M., 29, 30
Griggs, Sir Edward (Lord Altrincham), 3, 5, 31, 43-44, 45,
    49, 52, 53-55, 56, 57, 58, 59, 61, 131
Guggisberg, Sir Gordon, 3, 24, 44, 124
Gwandu, 109

Harcourt, Lord, 13, 16, 23
Hausa, 11, 18, 111, 124
Hehe, 35
Herbert, A. J., 28
Heussler, Robert, 78
Hill Angus, 124
Hilton Young Commission Report, 59-61

Ibadan, 10, 94, 106
Ibibio, 10, 17, 19-20, 29, 89, 91, 114, 119, 123, 127
Ibo, 10, 17, 19-20, 29, 89, 91, 114, 119, 123, 127
Idah, 99
Igala, 98
Ijaw, 10, 29, 91, 123
Ijebu-Ode, 108, 109
Ijemo Massacre, 19
Ilesha, 10
Imperial College of Agriculture, 129
Iringa Province, 70, 78
Isherwood, A. A., 83

Jackson, Thomas H., 110
Jaja of Opoba, 10
Johnson, Dr. Walter, 106

Johnston, J. Rooke, 7
Jumbe, 37-38

Kaduna, 111, 115
Kaleri, 124
Kano, 11, 106, 124
Kanuri, 96
Katsina, 106, 124
Kenya,
    closer union, 41-42, 44, 57 ff.; government of, 6, 31,
    43-44, 49, 52, 56, 57, 61, 132; Indian Community, 42,
    51, 61; labor, 42, 51; land policy, 51, 56, 57; white
    settlers, 31, 34, 36, 39-40, 65

Kilwa, 36
Kwanja system, 38

Lacey, A. Travers, 82
Lafia Emirate, 124
Lagos, 10, 28, 94, 95, 106, 109, 110-111, 118
Laibons, 78
Lawrence, C. T., 107
League of Nations, 31, 33, 34, 40, 53
Linfield, F. C., 42
Listowel, Judith, 6
Liwale, 37, 79
Llewellyn, Sir R. B., 16
Lloyd, Lord, 43
Lloyd-George, David, 43
Long, W. H. (Col. Sec.), 21
Lothain, Lord, 58
Lucas, Charles, 8, 9
Lugard, Edward, 14
Lugard, Lady (Flora Shaw), 14, 16
Lugard, Lord Frederick Delatry,
    amalgamation of Nigeria, 15-16; Northern Nigeria, 11,
    18, 95, 115-116; Tanganyika, 56-57, 61, 69, 72; taxation,
    29; as an administrator, 1, 3, 21, 23, 129; attitude
    toward anthropology, 17; disorders at Oyo, 19, 29;
    indirect rule in Nigeria, 16, 19, 22-23, 92, 115-116;
    Political Memoranda, 69; relations with Abeokuta, 19;
    relations with Cameron, 9, 12, 16, 20, 22, 33, 56-57,
    59, 89, 124-125; special position in Nigeria, 13-14

Lukikos, 77

Nsukka, 113
Hyamwezi, 35, 36
Nyasaland, 49

Ogbomosho, 10
Oil Rivers Protectorate, 10
Oloko, 92
Oldham, J. H., 59, 81
Onitsha Province, 123
Opobo, 10, 114
Ormsby-Gore, W. G. A., 41, 52, 81, 103
Ormsby-Gore Report, 41, 43, 44, 49
Owerri Province, 90, 103, 107, 113, 114, 119
Oyo, 10, 18-19, 93, 94

Palmer, Sir H. Richmond, 69, 91, 95
Passfield, Lord (Sidney Webb), 62, 65, 84, 87, 88, 93, 107,
    115
Peace Preservation Ordinance, 93, 107
Perham, Dame Margery, 1, 22, 83-84, 96, 101, 112, 124-125
Permanent Mandates Commission, 1, 34, 56, 84
Pinaar, Mr., 62
Plateau Province, 98
Plymouth, Earl of, 84
Principles of Native Administration, 125
Protectorate of Northern Nigeria, 11, 98
Protectorate of Southern Nigeria, 11, 98

Rabeh, 11
Richards, Sir Arthur, 125, 127
Riegels, William, 126-127
Rivers-Smith, Stanley, 81, 83
Ruanda-Urundi, 33, 35, 36, 37
Russell, Sir Alison, 81
Ruxton, Major U. F., 90-91

Sanusi, 110, 111
Sayers, G. S., 47, 130, 132
Schacht, Hjalmar, 53
Schuster, Sir George, 59
Scott, Sir John, 39, 46

Shambaa, 35
Sharwood-Smith, Sir Bryan, 127
Shendon Division, 124
Shepstone, Theophilus, 16
Sillery, Dr. Anthony, 130, 132
Smith, Captain, 48
Smuts, General Jan Christian, 33
Sokoto, 11, 109, 111, 124
Strachey, Charles, 53, 56
Sukuma, 70, 76
Sura District, 124
Swahili, 35
Swettenham, Frank, 23

Tabora, 35, 82, 122
Tabora Government School, 82
Talbot, P. Amaury, 90
Tanganyika Territory,
  agriculture, 41, 51; boundaries, 33-34; central government, 2, 6, 7, 31, 33-36, 48-49; closer union, 34, 40-41,
  44, 56 ff., 84; economic problems, 34-36, 46, 47; education, 80, 81-83; World War I, 33; German government, 33,
  36-38, 73, 79, 80; German landowners, 52-53; Indian community, 41, 60-61; indirect rule, 34-35, 47, 67 ff.;
  labor, 41, 50-51; land policy, 51, 53, 62-64; League of
  Nations, 33, 34, 40, 53; Legislative Council, 46-47, 86;
  Native Authority Ordinance, 1921, 72; Native Authority
  Ordinance, 1923, 72; Native Authority Ordinance, 1926,
  72-73, 80-81; Native Courts, 80-81; Native Treasuries,
  68; taxing systems, 38, 50, 67-68, 77; white settlers,
  35-36, 38, 41, 45, 47, 52-53, 62-64

Temple, Charles, 15, 16, 26
Thomas, J. H. (Col. Sec.), 31, 42, 64, 84
Thomson, Sir Graeme, 3, 23, 30, 31, 89, 90, 95, 100, 106, 115
Tiv, 98
Togo, 34
Tomlinson, G. J. F., 30, 91

Uchagga, 70
Uganda, 34, 49, 57, 60, 61, 65, 132
Unofficial White Settlers Conferences, 57, 60
Usambara, 70
Utu-Etim-Ekpo, 93

von Lettow-Vorbeck, General Paul, 33

Warrant Chiefs, 17, 19, 92, 114, 115, 119
Warri Province, 90, 106
Wesleyans, 81
Wilson, Sir Samuel, 53, 58, 61-62, 64-65

Yaba Higher College, 106
Yauri Emirate, 124
Yoruba, 10, 17, 93, 94
Young, Sir Hilton (Lord Kennet), 59-60

Zanzibar, 49
Zaria, 98, 124